Excreta Disposal in Emergencies

Excreta Disposal in Emergencies

A Field Manual

An Inter-Agency Publication

by Peter Harvey

with contributions from

Andy Bastable, Daudi Bikaba, Suzanne Ferron, Tim Forster,
Enamul Hoque, Sarah House, Leslie Morris, Mel Smith,
Lisette Verheijen and Vivien Walden.

WEDC

Water, Engineering and Development Centre,
Loughborough University,
Leicestershire
LE11 3TU UK

© WEDC/Practical Action Publishing Ltd, 2007

ISBN 978 1 84380 113 9

Harvey, P. A. (2007)
Excreta Disposal in Emergencies: A field manual
WEDC, Loughborough University, UK.

A catalogue record for this book is available from the British Library.

WEDC (The Water, Engineering and Development Centre) at Loughborough University in the UK is one of the world's leading institutions concerned with education, training, research and consultancy for the planning, provision and man-agement of physical infrastructure for development in low- and middle-income countries.

This edition reprinted and distributed by Practical Action Publishing.

Since 1974, Practical Action Publishing has published and disseminated books and information in support of international development work throughout the world. Practical Action Publishing trades only in support of its parent charity objectives and any profits are covenanted back to Practical Action (Charity Reg. No. 247257, Group VAT Registration No. 880 9924 76).

Printed on Demand

Acknowledgements

Project Steering Committee
Andy Bastable, Oxfam GB
Mark Henderson, UNICEF
Uli Jaspers, IFRC
Dinesh Shrestha, UNHCR

Designed and produced at WEDC by
Glenda McMahon and Rod Shaw

Illustrations
Ken Chatterton and Rod Shaw

The production of this manual was funded, supported and facilitated by the following organizations:

 International Federation
of Red Cross and Red Crescent Societies

 **Oxfam** unicef

Thanks are extended to the following individuals for contributing case study examples, photographs, additional information and review comments:

George Barreras, Frank Broadhurst, Stuart Cheesman, Sally Crook, St. John Day, Bill Fellows, Jean-Francois Fesselet, Jorge Figueroa, Robert Fraser, Mariona Miret Gaspa, Steve Harries, Ben Harvey, Dave Hockaday, Hazel Jones, Rajesh Kumar Pasupuleti, Bibi Lamond, Shamma Lal, Annie Lloyd, Richard Luff, Patrick Kilchenman, Jesee Wainaina Kinyanjui, Ali Marvasti, Victoria Murtagh, Jamila Nawaz, Joos van den Noortgate, Alban Nouvellon, Marion O'Reilly, Edoardo Piano, Jean-François Pinera, Manuel Quingani, Saira Raza, Bob Reed, Prasad Sevekari, Ann Smith, Zacarias Tchitumba, Alois Jost Widmer.

We also extend our thanks to the many agency staff who have also contributed to this manual.

Contents

List of boxes

List of figures

List of photographs

List of tables

1.
Introduction

It is generally accepted that excreta disposal is given less priority in emergencies than other humanitarian interventions such as health care, food and water supply. This is despite the fact that many of the most common diseases occurring in emergency situations are caused by inadequate sanitation facilities and poor hygiene practice. Many aid agencies are aware of these facts and wish to give a greater emphasis to excreta disposal. In the past, however, they have often been hampered by a lack of experience and resources to support their field staff.

1.1   About this manual

This manual is designed for use by field-based technicians, engineers and non-technical staff responsible for sanitation planning, management and intervention in emergencies. This may include international personnel sent to an emergency, local, national and regional staff.

The purpose of the manual is to provide practical guidance on how to select, design, construct and maintain appropriate excreta disposal systems to reduce faecal transmission risks and protect public health in emergency situations. Relevant situations include natural disasters, relief for refugees and Internally Displaced Persons (IDPs), and complex emergencies, focusing on rural and peri-urban areas.

The manual outlines the key issues to be considered when assessing excreta disposal needs and priorities, and provides guidance on how to plan, design and construct appropriate systems, and on how to maintain and promote appropriate use of those systems.

1.2 Excreta disposal, health and survival

Inadequate and unsafe disposal of human faeces can lead to the transmission of faeco-oral disease, can result in the contamination of the ground and water sources, and can provide breeding sites for flies and mosquitoes which may carry infection. In addition, faeces may attract domestic animals and vermin which spread the potential for disease. It can also create an unpleasant environment in terms of odour and sight.

While the provision of safe drinking water is also essential for the protection of public health, the importance of excreta disposal cannot be overestimated. Diarrhoeal diseases, transmitted via the faeco-oral route, account for 17 % of all deaths of children under five worldwide (WHO, 2006) and the risk of occurrence increase significantly in most emergency situations. In a refugee camp in Ethiopia in 1989, diarrhoeal disease was shown to account for 40% of all childhood deaths (Davis and Lambert, 2002), while among Rwandan refugees in Goma (Zaire) in 1994, more than 85% of all deaths in the initial emergency phase were associated with diarrhoeal diseases such as cholera and shigellosis (Médecins Sans Frontières, 1997). Studies (Fewtrell et al., 2005; Esrey, 1996) have shown that whilst improvements in water quality and quantity can produce limited reductions in childhood diarrhoea by 15 to 20%, greater reductions can be produced through safer excreta disposal (36%) and handwashing (35-42%).

Transmission of excreta-related diseases is largely faecal-oral or through skin penetration. Figure 1.1 illustrates the potential transmission routes for pathogens found in excreta.

The introduction of safe excreta disposal can reduce the incidence of intestinal infections and helminth infestations. Excreta-related communicable diseases include cholera, typhoid, dysentery (including shigellosis), diarrhoea, hookworm, schistosomiasis and filariasis (Franceys et al., 1992), as well as roundworms, poliomyelitis and hepatitis. The likelihood of all these diseases, and especially epidemics such as cholera, increases significantly when a population is displaced or affected by a disaster.

Poor hygiene practice, particularly involving food and hands, may be a major cause of disease transmission, even where appropriate excreta disposal facilities are in place. For this reason it is difficult to obtain a direct correlation between the incidence of excreta-related disease and the provision of appropriate facilities.

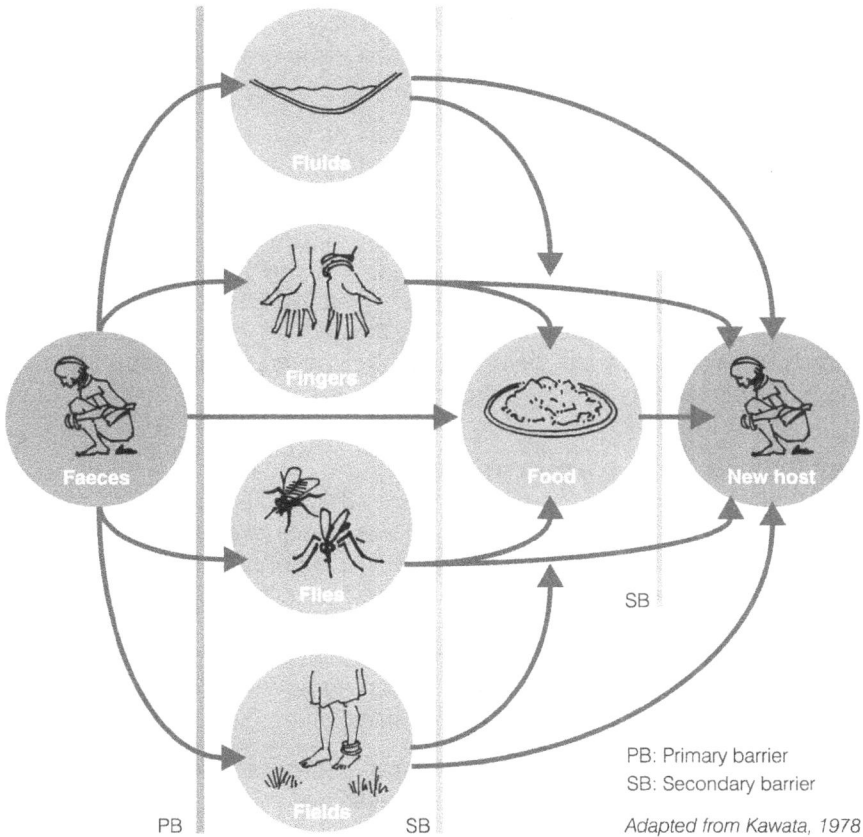

Figure 1.1. Faecal-oral transmission routes

Children under five years of age are most at risk from communicable diseases since their immune systems have not developed fully. Malnutrition resulting from food insecurity and chronic emergencies increases this risk further. Since young children are unaware of the health risks associated with contact with faeces, it is essential that faeces are safely contained. Severely malnourished children and adults are at increased risk from diarrhoeal disease, as are elderly people, especially if exhausted after travelling considerable distances.

1.3 Phases of an emergency

Davis and Lambert (2002) define three phases for an emergency:

- Immediate emergency
- Stabilization
- Recovery

For the purposes of excreta disposal applied to all types of emergency, these phases can be reduced to two: the 1st and 2nd phases. The 1st phase covers the immediate emergency phase and typically lasts from several weeks up to three months. The 2nd phase includes stabilization and recovery and may last several months or several years depending on the type and severity of the emergency.

1st Phase acute emergency

This is the immediate emergency phase where intervention is required to provide basic facilities to contain and separate excreta and to ensure survival. Response interventions are generally implemented rapidly and designed for short-term use. In this phase mortality rates are often high (over 1 per 10,000 per day) and the risk of major epidemics may also be high. In a large-scale population displacement (>20,000) the 1st phase typically lasts several weeks, though this may be more prolonged where response is slow or where the affected population increases rapidly.

The broad objective of an excreta disposal programme is to minimize high-risk practices and reduce faecal disease transmission rates. It should contribute to the health, dignity and general wellbeing of the affected community. Programmes should aim to achieve or surpass the Sphere minimum standards for excreta disposal (Sphere Project, 2004), but it is recognized that this may not be possible in the 1st phase of a large-scale emergency. The minimum standards should, however, be met during the 2nd phase.

2nd Phase stabilized emergency

The second emergency phase applies to all subsequent stages of an emergency, where the situation becomes stabilized and more sustainable interventions can be implemented for longer-term use. During this phase community structures may start to reassemble and morbidity and mortality rates should start to fall. However, the risk of epidemics may still be high. This typically lasts several months, though in complex emergencies it may stretch to several years.

The definition of these phases of an emergency is not fixed and many situations do not follow a linear progression. Some programmes may commence in the 2nd phase or become more acute and fall back to the 1st phase because the security situation deteriorates, the population increases, or an epidemic occurs.

1.4 Programme process

The overall programme process for excreta disposal in emergencies is summarized in Figure 1.2.

The process outlined is an expansion of the traditional project cycle that recognizes the unique conditions faced in many emergencies, that differ significantly from those encountered in more stable situations.

Rapid assessment is the initial assessment stage designed to gather key relevant information rapidly and analyze it quickly in order to prioritize intervention (see Checklist on page 11). This approach is designed to identify the need for immediate action as well as longer-term interventions.

Outline programme design follows on from the rapid assessment stage when a rapidly produced action plan is outlined. This identifies key actions that need to be implemented immediately to protect public health and stabilize the situation, as well as longer-term interventions, and is intended for submission to the donor for initial approval of the programme and budget.

Immediate action is the implementation of first-phase emergency measures to stabilize the current situation and minimize the spread of excreta-related disease. This may involve simple actions such as cleaning up after open defecation and providing basic separation and disposal facilities. It is important that the key longer-term actions have already been identified in the outline design to ensure that immediate actions do not have any negative effect on future interventions.

Follow-up assessment and consultation is a more detailed stage of data collection, analysis and consultation that should be carried out once the outline design has been approved. This should adopt a more participative approach involving all affected groups in the decision-making process.

Detailed programme design is a comprehensive plan of action for longer-term intervention (if required) based on the follow-up assessment and consultation process.

Implementation of the 2nd phase longer-term excreta disposal programme can now be conducted. This should include management and implementation of construction, hygiene promotion, operation and maintenance activities.

Monitoring and evaluation is the final stage in the assessment and planning process and is an ongoing process. All programme activities and the overall situation should be monitored to identify future needs and priorities, and to assess performance. On the basis of monitoring results it may be necessary to repeat the outline and detailed programme design stages leading to future immediate and longer-term interventions as required.

Rapid assessment and in-depth assessment and consultation are addressed in Chapter 2; outline programme design and detailed programme design are addressed in Chapter 3; immediate action is addressed in Chapter 4; implementation is addressed in Chapters 5, 6, 7 and 8; and monitoring is addressed in Chapter 9.

```
┌─────────────────────────────────────────┐
│            Rapid Assessment              │
└─────────────────────────────────────────┘
                    │
                    ▼
┌─────────────────────────────────────────┐
│          Outline Programme Design        │◄──────┐
└─────────────────────────────────────────┘       │
                    │                              │
                    ▼                              │
┌─────────────────────────────────────────┐       │
│         1st PHASE Immediate Action        │       │
└─────────────────────────────────────────┘       │
                    │                              │
                    ▼                              │
┌─────────────────────────────────────────┐       │
│     In-depth Assessment & Consultation    │       │
└─────────────────────────────────────────┘       │
                    │                              │
                    ▼                              │
┌─────────────────────────────────────────┐       │
│   Detailed Programme Design & Log-frame   │◄──────┤
└─────────────────────────────────────────┘       │
                    │                              │
                    ▼                              │
┌─────────────────────────────────────────┐       │
│   2nd PHASE Long-term Implementation      │       │
└─────────────────────────────────────────┘       │
                    │                              │
                    ▼                              │
┌─────────────────────────────────────────┐       │
│              Monitoring                   │───────┘
└─────────────────────────────────────────┘
```

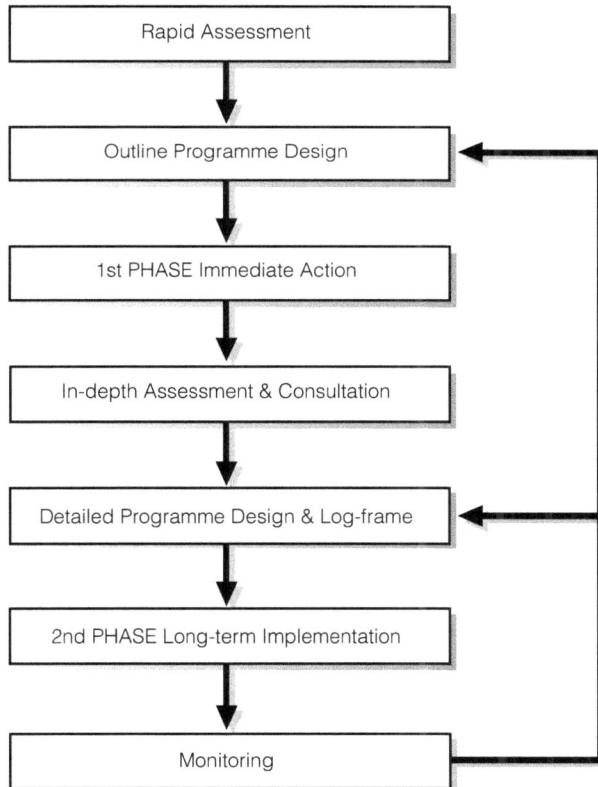

Figure 1.2. Programme process for emergencies

2.

Assessment

CONSULTATION with the affected community is an ESSENTIAL part of the assessment process, even in an acute emergency. This is important to ensure that excreta disposal facilities are used and maintained.

2.1 Assessment principles

The importance of assessment should not be underestimated. Even in an acute emergency, assessment is the cornerstone of a successful excreta disposal response programme. Assessment involves the collection and analysis of a variety of information and data. The key points to remember when undertaking assessments are:

- Key information should be collected from as many different people and sources as possible to corroborate findings. Additional data may be collected after decisions have been made for confirmation.

- It is essential to understand local political and social structures and to be aware of conflicting interests and biases within communities when collecting information. It is also important to discuss the purpose of the assessment with communities to avoid raising expectations unrealistically.

- Communities' preferences regarding excreta disposal practices and facilities must be understood if facilities are to be used and have the desired impact on public health (see Box 2.1).

- Collect *enough* data to implement an effective response. Time spent collecting unnecessary information is time wasted. Focus on the most relevant factors (the checklist provided on page 11 can assist in this).

- Keep good records of any gathered information and store them in such a way that others can access them.
- Remember that in most situations things are constantly changing, it is important, therefore, to look at both the present situation and what is likely to happen in the near future.

Box 2.1.

The importance of consulting communities

Latrines provided in a refugee camp in Eastern Chad in 2004 were not used by the camp population as they were not happy with the design or location of facilities.

Simple dry pit latrines provided for Kosovan refugees in Albania in 1999 and for communities affected by the Asian tsunami in 2004, were not used by either population due to a common desire to use water-based (pour-flush) latrines only.

Such low levels of acceptability and non-use of latrines can be avoided through thorough consultation with communities, both to determine their existing practices and preferences, and to involve them in the planning and implementation process for excreta disposal and related hygiene promotion activities.

The rapid assessment and follow-up assessment stages must address a number of key issues, as outlined in the following sections. Twenty key questions to be applied when collecting baseline data in initial assessments are presented on page 11. These are generic and may not all be relevant in all emergency situations. The question 'so what?' is a useful test of relevance – ask it frequently (Davis and Lambert, 2002).

Twenty Rapid Assessment Questions

1. What is the estimated population and what is the population density?

2. What is the crude mortality rate (number of deaths per 10,000 people per day) and what are the main causes of mortality and morbidity?

3. How did people dispose of excreta before the emergency? What are the current beliefs and traditions concerning excreta disposal especially regarding women and children's excreta? (do men and women or all family members share latrines, can women be seen walking to a latrine, do children use potties, is children's excreta thought to be safe?)

4. Will people who traditionally use water-seal latrines accept direct-drop dry systems in the short-term? Is there sufficient water available for water-seal latrines to be provided?

5. What material/water is used for anal-cleansing? Is it available? Is soap available?

6. Are there any existing facilities? If so, are they used, are they sufficient and are they operating successfully? Can they be extended or adapted? Do all groups have equal access to these facilities?

7. Are the current defecation practices a threat to health? If so, how?

8. What is the current level of awareness of public health risks?

9. Are there any public health promotion activities taking place? Who is involved in these activities?

10. What health promotion media are available/accessible to the affected population?

11. Are men, women and children prepared to use defecation fields, communal latrines or family latrines? Consult people with disabilities and those who are elderly.

12. Is there sufficient space for defecation fields, pit latrines etc.?

13. What are the topography and drainage patterns of the area?

14. What is the depth and permeability of the soil, and can it be dug easily?

15. What is the level of the groundwater-table?

16. What local materials are available for constructing latrines?

17. Are there any people familiar with the construction of latrines?

18. How do women deal with menstruation? Are there materials or facilities they need for this?

19. When does the seasonal rainfall occur?

20. Whose role is it normally to construct, pay for, maintain and clean a latrine (men, women or both)?

Health and hygiene issues

The primary purpose of an excreta disposal programme in emergencies is to sustain or improve health by minimizing the transmission of disease-causing pathogens. Health and hygiene issues, therefore, have particular relevance when conducting any assessment. These are especially important in order to determine the key risks to the affected population and, consequently, to identify intervention priorities.

The current health status of the affected population and potential threats to health are key assessment indicators. Excreta-related diseases include, among others:

- diarrhoea
- bacillary dysentery
  (shigellosis)
- Hepatitis (A,C,E)
- cholera
- cryptosporidiosis
- roundworm

In an emergency situation Crude Mortality Rate (CMR), in deaths per 10,000 people per day, is the most practical indicator of the health status of a population. As long as the CMR remains above 1 death /10,000/day the situation is generally classed as an emergency (Sphere, 2004).

Morbidity rates for excreta-related disease can also be useful indicators. Although it is not possible to provide 'acceptable' incidence rates for different diseases (Rottier and Ince, 2003), it is recommended that figures should be lower than those presented in Table 2.1.

Where clinical data are available these should be assessed to determine the relative prevalence of diseases to help identify key risks and priorities. Consultation with medical staff early on is an important step to determine the most severe or unusual morbidity rates. An understanding of the local context is especially important as some diseases may be endemic and relatively high morbidity rates for these may not be unusual.

Hygiene promoters working in emergency situations have an important role in assessing social indicators as well as clinical data. Social indicators include hygiene behaviour and cultural practices, as well as aspects of vulnerability such as age, gender, disability and pre-existing ill health.

Transmission of excreta-related diseases is exacerbated by lack of appropriate hygiene practices, such as handwashing after defecation, disposal of children's faeces, and regular cleaning of latrines.

Table 2.1. Indicative acceptable incidence rates in camps for displaced persons or refugees (after de Veer, 1998)

Disease	Incidence rate (in cases/10,000/week)
Diarrhoea total	60
Acute watery diarrhoea	50
Bloody diarrhoea	20
Cholera	Every suspected case must be acted upon

A lack of baseline information on hygiene behaviour can lead to project failure. While it is difficult to assess whether all sections of the population are aware of priority hygiene practices, it is always useful to conduct a small study on issues such as handwashing and disposal of children's faeces (see Box 2.2).

HIV/AIDS is also of particular relevance to excreta disposal in emergency situations. Poor sanitation raises particular risks for people living with AIDS as their weakened immune systems are less resistant to opportunistic infections. The HIV/AIDS epidemic is, therefore, increasing the need to provide sanitation and improve hygiene practices because diarrhoea and skin diseases are among the most common opportunistic infections. Poor hygiene and sanitation is one of the leading causes of the progression of asymptotic HIV to AIDS. For some patients, diarrhoea can become chronic, weakening them and often resulting in death.

Particularly in countries where HIV prevalence is high, assessments should be conducted taking into account the extreme vulnerability of adults living with HIV/AIDS. Emergencies occurring against a backdrop of high HIV prevalence challenge all response groups to revise their hitherto accepted mode of response. However, any attempt to collect information about known HIV-positive people, or target assistance specifically for them, should be approached with caution to avoid stigmatizing them. Even in communities where prevalence rates are known to be high, it is often unacceptable to discuss this openly. Asking about the chronically sick may be more acceptable and contacting them through local HIV/AIDS organizations should be considered where possible.

Box 2.2.

**The importance of incorporating baseline
information on hygiene behaviour in Eritrea**

In Eritrea, the Ministry of Health did some research on health
behaviours in the IDP camps (Deda, Mai Haber and Adi Keshi) in
September 2000. The results showed that the residents knew a
great deal about health problems in their camps and knew about the
causes of health problems. However, based on formative research
on the health behaviours in selected IDP camps, it was concluded
that 'there exists a great gap between what people know and what
they do.' Research identified problems with using latrines, 'in spite
of the efforts made to provide latrines in the camps.' The potties
that had been distributed by the agency were not being used and
children's defecation was observed everywhere.

Following on from this research an Information, Education and
Communication (IEC) strategy was drafted for the IDP camps
by the Ministry of Health. This was presented in a tabulated
form, with the problem behaviour matched to factors promoting
problem behaviour and factors supporting behaviour change.
This information was used to help guide the excreta disposal
programme, particularly concerning health behaviour.

Socio-cultural issues

Excreta disposal provision is essentially people-centred and the importance of socio-cultural issues is paramount if programmes are to be
successful. Relevant socio-cultural issues to consider in assessments
include:

- population and demography – numbers of men, women and
  children, breakdown by age, ethnic and religious groups, population
  density;

- vulnerability and disability – numbers of people with physical and mental disabilities or sickness, most vulnerable groups;

- cultural beliefs, practices and preferences relating to excreta disposal and hygiene (e.g. menstruation);

- existing knowledge relating to health and hygiene;

- anatomical considerations (e.g. how people squat); and

- anal-cleansing materials.

Such information is essential to set up a baseline for an effective excreta disposal programme.

Women are potential agents of change in hygiene education, and children are the most vulnerable victims, but men usually make the decisions about whether to tackle the problem, and how. Women often need privacy and security in sanitation more than men, yet they are unable to express those needs effectively in many societies.

Plans for designing and locating sanitation facilities must consider cultural issues, particularly as excreta disposal is usually focused on the household. Excreta disposal may be a difficult subject for a community to discuss: it may be taboo, or people may not like to discuss issues they regard as personal and unclean. In some cases, people may feel that facilities are not appropriate for children, or that children's faeces are not harmful. Such issues need to be addressed with sensitivity at an early stage. This is essential to ensure that interventions are appropriate, facilities will be used and people affected by emergencies maintain their dignity.

Environmental and technical issues

The range of technical options that can be applied in any particular situation will depend both on the human environment and the physical environment in which the emergency occurs. Environmental and technical issues to consider in assessments include:

- ground conditions – soil types and infiltration rates (see Appendix 1), groundwater levels, bearing capacity of soil, ease of excavation;

- location and risk of contamination of water sources;

- topography and drainage patterns;
- climate and rainfall patterns;
- natural, physical and human resources (and skills) available locally or that can be procured rapidly; and
- possible environmental constraints or impacts.

2.2 Assessment tools and techniques

Field assessments can incorporate a variety of techniques, including:

- observation;
- measurement and testing;
- surveys;
- interviews; and
- participatory techniques.

Observation

Perhaps the simplest way of gathering information is through observation. This method allows the assessor to record non-verbal behaviour among the affected population, the physical condition of the affected area and the characteristics of the surrounding landscape. It can also explore interactions among the affected population and local residents or other stakeholders.

On arrival in the field the first step in assessment is to conduct a rapid reconnaissance of the affected area. This is best done on foot and may be a useful starting point in producing a simple sketch map. Transect walks can be made through the site to take notes on any existing excreta disposal facilities and practices and associated indicators. A huge amount of information can be gathered in this way but care should be taken not to make sweeping assumptions based on limited observation.

It should be noted that observation methods based on people's behaviour are subjective and time consuming. They cannot detect what members of the affected population are thinking, and the presence of an outsider can change the behaviour of those being observed.

Measurement and testing

Measurements can be used to determine quantities such as:

* available area;

* geographical position;

* elevation and slopes;

* level of water-table;

* latrine superstructure dimensions for existing facilities or materials;

* quantity of water available for handwashing / anal-cleansing;

* ease of excavation for pits; and

* soil infiltration rates.

Measurements are likely to require the data collector to have some skill and experience in using appropriate instruments. Assessment teams can be trained reasonably quickly for most measurements, but should be carefully supervised throughout data collection.

Surveys

Surveys can be used to examine opinions or behaviour by asking people set questions. Surveys can be used to collect both quantitative and qualitative information. This may be quantitative statistical data concerning demography, health and geography, or qualitative social data such as community opinions and behaviour. There is a broad range of survey techniques which can be used for emergency sanitation programmes, including random and selective methods. The use of surveys should be balanced against available time, human resources, logistical support, and the need for statistical analysis and interpretation of results. In the 1st phase emergency it may only be possible to collect information that is representative of the situation rather than statistically valid. Comprehensive surveys may be more appropriate for detailed follow-up assessments than for rapid assessments.

Interviews

Since excreta disposal is essentially a people-centred sector, not all information can be gathered through observation. Even in the initial rapid assessment it will be necessary to interview some groups and individuals.

There are various interview techniques ranging from open-ended discussion with randomly selected members of the affected population to more directed interviews with key informants or personnel from NGOs. Care should be taken in conducting interviews; the assessor should avoid asking leading questions (where the desired answer is obvious) or restrictive questions (with yes or no answers only). Interviewees can include:

- key informants (engineers, teachers, health staff etc.);
- men, women and children from the affected population;
- formal leaders; and
- representatives of minority or vulnerable groups.

Women and children, as well as men, should be questioned. Where translators are needed, female translators should be used where possible in interviewing women, especially in cultures where women's contact with men is restricted. Appropriate local staff should be used wherever possible.

It is important to remember that in some situations, interviewers and observers may pose a threat to the people, interpreters and authorities concerned. Rapid assessment teams can compromise these groups by asking the wrong questions or quoting their answers to the wrong person (Gosling and Edwards, 1995).

To obtain in-depth information about practices and beliefs it may be useful to undertake participatory techniques, such as a community mapping session, with separate male and female groups. Community members will then be able to give you important information about where there are problems with excreta disposal, what sort of toilets most people have, where people dispose of children's faeces and what possible solutions people would like to see.

Participatory techniques

There are many participatory techniques that can be used in assessment, although experienced staff are needed to conduct most of these. The most common at the raid assessment stage are group discussion and community mapping. Group discussions may be opportunistic with whichever people are encountered during the assessment, or may involve focus groups. Focus group discussions need to be pre-planned and usually involve a more homogenous group of people who are guided by the assessor through a detailed discussion on specific issues. These groups generally work better where participants are of the same sex and similar in age. Single-sex focus groups may promote greater freedom of expression by participants who may not want to express their opinion in a mixed group.

Discussions are semi-structured and the assessor will introduce a list of topics to encourage wider discussion among the group's members. This will enable the facilitator to learn about their concerns, opinions, problems, and what they consider to be priorities.

Mapping is a useful exercise which can be used to gain an overview of the situation and to identify excreta disposal problems which are causing a risk to people's health. A mapping exercise should also allow people themselves to appreciate possible risks and can often be a catalyst for community planned action. This can build on the observation process during the initial reconnaissance by sketching site plans or schematic maps. This may be used to record locations of:

- existing sanitation facilities and practices;
- key public services and institutions;
- open defecation;
- standing water;
- water sources, storage and distribution points; and
- slopes, drainage and geological features.

Mapping can be carried out relatively quickly by community members in conjunction with local staff. This is another way of stimulating discussion and obtaining information on a wide range of issues from those present. Maps (no matter how rough) can be very useful in co-ordination and planning meetings with other individuals, organizations and agencies.

Whatever technique is adopted, care must be taken during the initial rapid assessment that the expectations of the affected community are not raised unduly prior to programme approval.

A guide explaining how to conduct a mapping exercise is presented in the box on page 20.

How to conduct a mapping exercise

A mapping exercise can be initiated simply by approaching a small group of people or by organizing groups of people in advance. It is useful to conduct separate mapping exercises with women and men to ascertain their different views.

- Have a clear idea in your mind of the possible things that might be identified on a map such as church, market place, schools, areas of open defecation, houses or shelters without latrines, areas of fly breeding etc.

- Identify possible resources that might be used for the map such as stones, leaves etc. but allow people to make their suggestions as you go along.

- Explain who you are and that you would like their help in conducting the exercise.

- Explain what you hope to find out and how the participants might go about making a map.

- Allow plenty of time for discussion of the idea of making a map - many people may be sceptical that they cannot do this because they have never been to school.

- If necessary begin the process yourself with a central landmark using a stick to draw on the ground. Try to 'hand over the stick' as much as possible to other participants.

- Listen carefully to what people say and allow free discussion and debate amongst participants.

- Keep a record of who took part and when and where.

- When the map is finished, offer to transcribe it or get one of the participants to transcribe it onto paper. Ask the participants to decide where they would like the map to be kept, or who will keep it.

It might also be useful to compile quantifiable data from the mapping exercise. A table showing the quantities of each thing that has been drawn on the map (i.e. numbers of latrines in different locations) can then provide a baseline for subsequent quantifiable evaluation or for the triangulation of results from questionnaire surveys. This can also be displayed with the map for those who can read.

2.3 Follow-up assessment and consultation

Assessment is not simply a one-stage process. The initial rapid assessment is designed to collect key information quickly in order to prioritize intervention activities and produce an outline programme design. The assessment tools and techniques described above can be applied at any stage of an excreta disposal programme, and techniques used in the initial assessment can be revisited and repeated in the follow-up assessment.

Once the outline programme design has been produced and immediate actions are implemented to stabilize the initial situation, a follow-up assessment and consultation process should begin in order to gather more comprehensive information and produce a detailed programme design.

This more in-depth consultation phase takes time but is essential to ensure that interventions and facilities are socio-culturally acceptable, and that they will be operated and maintained effectively. Participative tools are very useful to find out more about the 'why' rather than just the 'what' people do. Triangulation of information collected with different tools and approaches is important in order to obtain a more in-depth understanding of the situation for baseline data to be used to set benchmarks for monitoring.

More detailed information on different assessment techniques that can be employed can be found in Ferron, Morgan & O'Reilly (2006) *Hygiene Promotion: From relief to development*. Intermediate Technology Development Group Publishing: UK.

3.
Programme Design

Effective planning and design is the key to the success of any excreta disposal programme. The OUTLINE programme design should identify the immediate objectives, priorities and actions, and the DETAILED programme design should define the longer-term objectives and activities based on detailed consideration of technical and social factors.

3.1 Outline programme design

The objective of the outline programme design is to use the information collected in the initial assessment to set objectives for intervention, identify intended outputs and outline the key activities required to achieve these. Every programme should have (a) clear:

- **Goal** – the overall aim of intervention (e.g. to sustain or improve the health and well-being of the affected population);

- **Purpose** – the reason for implementing an excreta disposal programme (e.g. to reduce the incidence of excreta-related disease and create a pleasant living environment);

- **Outputs** – the key objectives that should be met by the programme (e.g. to ensure adequate excreta disposal in line with Sphere minimum standards);

- **Activities** – the actions required to achieve the outputs (e.g. latrine construction, hygiene promotion); and

- **Inputs** – the resources required to implement the activities identified (e.g. raw materials, tools, equipment, finances, personnel).

Setting objectives

The objectives of any excreta disposal programme must be clear from the onset. These will be similar in most emergency situations, and linked to the overall programme goal of sustaining or improving the health and well-being of the affected population, and the purpose of reducing the incidence of excreta-related disease and creating a pleasant living environment.

Typical immediate objectives include:

- to ensure containment of human excreta and separation from food and water sources;
- to ensure that all sections of the community have access to safe and acceptable excreta disposal facilities; and
- to ensure that community members are aware of what they can do to minimize immediate health risks and are mobilized to take action.

Setting priorities

Once the overall output objectives have been decided upon, the priority 1st phase intervention activities must be identified. These should be based on the **key public health risks** that affect the largest number of people (identified during the assessment process) and, consequently, determination of the **immediate chronic needs**.

There is a common tension between starting to construct facilities as soon as possible to meet urgent needs in high-risk situations – and the need to have at least minimal consultation with the affected community to determine priorities and preferences. Needs and priorities will be context-specific and each setting must be assessed fully. Several activities may start at the same time or may need to continue into the next phase of the programme. Some examples of typical activities are presented below, though these will not be appropriate in all situations.

- It may be necessary to immediately start a clean-up campaign if there has been open defecation which is causing an obvious health hazard. The population can be mobilized, using rapidly identified and recruited public health promoters (community mobilizers) and given the resources (lime, spades, wheelbarrows, sacks) to mobilize people to do the clean-up. It may be necessary to pay workers to do this, but care should be taken in making such decisions, since once people have been paid it will be more difficult to mobilize voluntary participation for other programme activities.

- In the 1st phase of an emergency, public health promoters would also need to initiate an information exchange. The people need to be informed about where they can and cannot defecate and why indiscriminate defecation is a problem in areas of high population density. They may also need to be reminded of the importance of handwashing especially following defecation and after handling children's stools.

- As part of the sanitation team, the public health promoters also need to obtain information about which system of excreta disposal is most appropriate and where facilities should be sited. As soon as possible, find out about social norms and preferences and feed this information into construction plans.

- If appropriate, start shallow trench defecation enclosures immediately, while beginning the planning for communal or family latrine construction (see Chapter 4 for more details).

- Consider whether there need to be special facilities for children through discussions with the public health promoters.

- Dig a number of trial pits around the camp to determine: soil stability and permeability, depth to bedrock and depth to water-table. This will influence the decision to build lined or unlined pits, raised latrines or to go for more technical solutions such as septic-tanks, small sewage systems or small treatment systems.

- If appropriate, start building communal latrines and ensure that latrine attendants have been selected and trained.

- It may be possible to initiate a family latrine programme at the same time as providing a minimum of communal latrines – if families are willing to dig latrine pits themselves. They may want to borrow tools for digging. This aspect of the programme could be managed by the public health promoters.

- It is also important to consider whether it is possible to upgrade any existing sanitation facilities in the location.

Action plan

An action or activity plan (see Table 3.1) must be developed once the key priorities have been decided. Each activity should be allotted an appropriate time period to produce a schedule for the initial stage of the programme in the form of a Gantt chart.

Table 3.1. Example activity plan

Activities	Week number					
	1	2	3	4	5	6
Recruit and train five mobile sanitation teams – each with a supervisor – to organize excreta clean-up within three days of arrival	▓					
Recruit and orientate five public health promoters to collect baseline data and information about community latrine-design preferences	▓					
Establish communal latrine system for entire population within two weeks including handwashing facilities and trained latrine attendants	▓	▓				
Hold regular community meetings with camp leaders and representatives (ensuring representation from women, elderly and disabled) to discuss family latrine programme and operation and maintenance	▓	▓	▓	▓	▓	▓
Distribute potties to each family with children aged between one and five (one potty for every two children) and nappies for children under one (four nappies per child)		▓	▓	▓	▓	▓
Establish family pit latrines for 10,000 families within two months ensuring privacy and safety for women			▓	▓	▓	▓

Immediate action

Once the outline programme design has been drawn up to produce a rough plan for the overall programme, immediate action should be taken. Such action should entail the implementation of first-phase technical options (as described in Chapter 4). The outline design should be produced within one or two days to avoid any unnecessary delay in implementing emergency measures. It is important, however, that longer-term objectives are clearly defined before rushing headlong into action, to minimize mistakes and ensure that time and resources are used efficiently.

While immediate action is underway, the outline programme design can, if necessary, be submitted to the donor or agency headquarters for approval.

3.2 Detailed programme design

The detailed programme design is an extension of the outline design which contains more detail regarding activities, designs, materials, resources and timeframes, especially for the longer term. While immediate emergency measures are being implemented the outline design should be expanded to produce a more comprehensive plan of action for second-phase interventions. The foundation of this should be a logical framework.

Logical framework

The logical framework is a useful planning tool which is increasingly required by donors to ensure that objectives are well-defined. Its use can also encourage more effective monitoring and evaluation and ensures a more rigorous and accountable approach to emergency response. In a rapidly changing environment, it is accepted that such a framework will be less than perfect and may need to change frequently to accommodate the situation on the ground.

The example logical framework in Table 3.2 assumes a population of 50,000 newly displaced people in a camp setting and considers the excreta disposal requirements only. In reality, close co-ordination and collaboration would also be needed with those involved in the provision of water and health services. Key design criteria based on Sphere Minimum Standards (Sphere, 2004) have been used to promote familiarity but output objectives should be more specific if presenting this framework to donors. Activities and inputs should be defined more comprehensively during the detailed design process and form the basis of a more detailed action plan for the longer-term.

Table 3.2. Example logical framework

Narrative summary	Measurable indicators	Means of verification	Key assumptions
Aim/Goal:			
To contribute to improving the health of the at-risk population.	Crude Mortality Rate and morbidity rates from all causes (where possible)	Clinical data Community surveys	Assumes that stability is maintained and that further migration does not take place, assumes easy access to population.
Purpose:			
To reduce the incidence of diseases associated with inadequate excreta disposal for population X for Y months.	Mortality and morbidity rates from diarrhoeal diseases (though other external factors may affect morbidity rates) Proxy indicators: • acceptability of facilities • use of facilities • perceived improvements	Clinical data Community surveys Latrine monitoring forms Observation Pocket voting Focus group discussions (FGDs)	Assumes that the major cause or risk of mortality and morbidity is associated with excreta-related disease and that community members see the project as a priority need for them.

Table 3.2. Example logical framework continued ....

Narrative summary	Measurable indicators	Means of verification	Key assumptions
Output:			
To ensure adequate excreta disposal in line with Sphere minimum standards within six months. All sections of the community are enabled to practice safer hygiene in a dignified and culturally appropriate manner.	• 1 latrine constructed per 20 people after community consultation OR 1 latrine per household • No faecal matter observed in the target area • Hand washing facilities at all latrines and are maintained • Each household reports the presence of soap on random weekly visits	Latrine monitoring forms Reports by latrine assistants Observation Weekly random transect walk Random household visits Handwashing demonstrations with children	Assumes government support for project continues and land is available for the construction of latrines Assumes project meets a felt need of the community
Activities:			
1. Recruit & train personnel 2. Design & construct latrines 3. Monitor programme activities and indicators .... etc.	Numbers of staff and training completed Etc...	Project records, training evaluation Etc...	Assumes availability of willing/able people Etc..
Inputs:			
	Tools and resources	Logistics and financial records	Resources and finances are rapidly available

Key design criteria for excreta disposal

(Based on the Sphere Minimum Standards in Hygiene, Water Supply and Sanitation, Sphere, 2004)

Coverage

Sphere indicator: **Maximum of 20 people per latrine** (in the initial phase it is reasonable to aim for 50 p/p/latrine).

Trench latrines should be designed for a maximum of 100 people per 3.5m length of trench at 1m deep and 300mm wide.

Separate toilets may need to be provided for women and men, the distances to which should be determined following consultation with the intended users. Toilets and facilities for people living with disabilities, the elderly and children should also be provided.

Location

Toilets should be **no more than 50m from dwellings**. Pit latrines should be a minimum of 6m from dwellings. Latrines should be at least 30m from any groundwater sources. Latrines should be available in public places such as markets, health centres and food/non-food distribution points.

Pit depth

The bottom of the latrine should be **at least 1.5m above the water-table**. In fine unsaturated soils and unconsolidated strata within 1.5m, virtually all bacteria, viruses and other faecal organisms are removed. This distance will increase in large-grained soils, gravels or fissured/fractured rock.

Accumulation rates

Sludge accumulation rates are useful indicators for designing and sizing pits for excreta. Approximate rates are given below:

Solids: 0.5 litres/person/day in emergencies ($<0.15m^3$/person/year in stable situations)

Liquid: 0.8 litres/person/day where water is not used for anal-cleansing or 1.3 l/p/d where water is used for anal-cleansing.

Note: Where there are no bathing facilities people may wash in latrines, in which case the accumulation rate could be 8–10 l/p/d.

User issues

All latrine doors should be lockable from the inside. Handwashing facilities and, if necessary, water or other materials for anal-cleansing should also be provided. There should be a ratio of 3:1 for female to male cubicles. Special rails, access ramps and larger cubicle spaces may also be necessary to assist disabled, elderly or chronically sick people. Provision of spaces for washing and drying menstruation cloths may also be necessary.

3.3   Planning for the needs of people

It is essential that the detailed programme design incorporates the needs of the different groups of people within an affected community. This may include consideration of ethnic and family groups, age, gender, disability, and ill health. This can only be achieved through active and ongoing consultation with all relevant groups within the community.

Dignity

Although protecting public health is usually the primary purpose for ensuring safe excreta disposal in emergencies, there are also other reasons as to why this is important. Not least is the provision and enhancement of dignity. Dignity is an inherent characteristic of being human, it can be subjectively felt as an attribute of the self, and is made manifest through behaviour that demonstrates respect for self and others (Jacelon et al., 2004). Excreta disposal programmes can, therefore, affect the dignity of users, both in the way in which they are designed and the way in which they are implemented. Some key aspects of programmes that enhance human dignity are:

- **Mutual respect** – programmes should be planned and implemented in a way that does not treat beneficiaries as helpless dependants, but as equal human beings.

- **Empowerment** – community members should be consulted in the programme design process and given decision-making opportunities.

- **Essential-means provision** – affected people should be provided with essential means to ensure personal and family hygiene.

- **Privacy** – excreta disposal facilities must provide sufficient privacy, especially for women and girls.

- **Accessibility** – facilities must be accessible to all, including the very young, very old, chronically sick and disabled people; they must also be located where risks to personal safety are minimized.

- **Cultural sensitivity** – consultation and planning approaches should show respect for traditional community leadership structures and practices.

Family or communal facilities

In many emergency situations it is necessary to make a choice between providing family, communal or shared excreta disposal facilities. Field experience tends to indicate that the fewer people there are per facility, the greater the involvement of that population in O&M activities. Consequently, it is widely accepted that family facilities are, in general, preferable to communal facilities. In the initial stages of an emergency, however, it is often necessary to construct communal latrines, as there is insufficient time to implement family-based facilities. However, due to management and maintenance problems associated with communal services, communal latrines are normally seen as only a short-term measure before family latrines can be built, or for use in public places such as markets, food and health centres.

Family toilets

Where possible, it is preferable, in order to promote ownership, care and maintenance, for family members to build their own latrines. In some cases the population may be rapidly mobilized to dig their own family pit latrines, and there may be no need for communal facilities even in the initial phase of an emergency.

If community members are to build their own latrines, it may be necessary to provide tools and equipment and additional help to those who may be unable to do this, such as female-headed households, families with disabilities, and the elderly. In many cases, families are given latrine slabs and are expected to construct the pit and superstructure themselves, using local materials.

Communal facilities

In some initial disaster situations, especially where there is limited space or resources, and in public places, it is necessary to construct toilets for communal use. In such situations it is very important to establish systems for the effective regular cleaning and maintenance of these facilities. Responsibility for O&M of communal latrines is often the source of tension or resentment, especially where this relies on voluntary inputs and, as a result, facilities may not be adequately maintained – leading to increased health hazards.

It is likely that in the following scenarios communal latrines will be the most appropriate or only option:

- hard shelters (schools, public buildings, factory buildings, emergency centres);

- enclosed centres (prisons, hospitals, orphanages, feeding centres etc.);

- difficult physical conditions (e.g. rocky ground, high water-table level);

- over-crowded peri-urban areas;

- crowded camps with little available space (population density >300 per hectare);

- transit camps where facilities are temporary; and

- where the local authorities do not permit family units.

It is usually necessary to employ people to maintain and clean communal latrines, as it is difficult to encourage users to undertake this on a purely voluntary basis.

Shared facilities

An effective compromise between family and communal facilities is the provision of shared facilities whereby one toilet is shared by four or five families. Where the families have been consulted about its siting and design, and have the responsibility and the means to clean and maintain it, a shared facility is generally better kept, cleaner and, therefore, more regularly used than a communal facility. It is important to organize access to shared facilities by working with the intended users to decide who will have access to the toilet and how it will be cleaned and maintained. Efforts should be made to provide easy access to facilities for disabled people and those living with HIV/AIDS.

There are many advantages and disadvantages of both communal and family latrines. The final decision will depend on a variety of factors as outlined in Table 3.3.

Table 3.3. Advantages and disadvantages of communal and family latrines

Factor	Communal	Family
Speed of construction	Can be constructed fast by well-trained and well-equipped team, although rate of construction limited by number of staff and equipment.	May take considerable time to train families in the initial stages, but large numbers of latrines may be built quickly.
Technical quality	Quality of design and construction easier to control but innovative ideas from users may be missed.	Potential for innovative ideas of users, but more difficult to ensure good siting and construction.
Construction costs	Use of materials can be easily controlled but labour must be paid for.	Construction labour and some materials free of charge; families may not have time or skills.
Maintenance costs	Maintenance, repair and replacement costs easier to predict and plan; staff required to clean and maintain facilities in long-term.	Users take responsibility for cleaning and maintenance but recurrent costs are less predictable.
Technical possibilities	Heavy equipment and specialized techniques may be used where necessary (e.g. rocky ground).	Families may not be able to dig in hard rock or build raised pit latrines where the water-table is high.
Cleaning and hygiene	Users do not have to clean latrines, but these are often dirty, and a greater mix of users increases the risk of disease transmission.	Latrines are often cleaner but many users may prefer not to be responsible for construction, cleaning and maintenance.
Access and security	Latrines may be less accessible and more insecure, particularly for women.	Latrines are often more accessible (closer to dwellings) and safer.
Development issues	People may lose or not acquire the habit of looking after their own latrine.	People keep or develop the habit of managing their own latrine.

Source: adapted from Adams, 1999

Gender considerations

Emergency interventions and life-saving strategies have a greater impact when there is understanding of different gender impacts, and of men and women's different needs, interests, vulnerabilities, capacities and coping strategies. The equal rights of men and women are explicit in the Humanitarian Charter. Rights and opportunities for both men and women should be enhanced and not compromised by aid interventions. Increased protection from violence, coercion and deprivation in emergency situations, particularly for women and girls, but also for specific risks faced by men and boys, are essential to effective emergency relief.

It is also important to pay attention to the impact of programmes on women's roles and workloads, access to and control of resources, decision making powers, and opportunities for skill development, in order to make sure that interventions support and do not diminish the role of women.

Excreta disposal is a sensitive socio-cultural issue and in many societies there are particular cultural beliefs relating to excreta disposal practices and facilities. In some cases the sharing of facilities by people of different gender is a taboo, even within family groups. Where possible latrines should be segregated by sex and there should be a typical **ratio of 3:1 for female to male latrines.**

There is also often a need for facilities and resources for menstruation which must be considered when providing latrines. Some issues to consider with respect to menstruation are as follows:

1. Ask women and girls about how they normally deal with their menstrual periods.

2. In a camp situation, sanitary pads can be provided, but should be avoided where possible because of the risks of inappropriate disposal. Where they are the only culturally appropriate solution care must be taken to ensure that correct disposal options are discussed and provided (burning / incinerating / burying).

3. The problem with using cloth which is washable in a camp environment is that once used the cloth needs washing and drying. Unless a specific space – that has a degree of privacy – is made available for this, it will be very difficult for women to dry their sanitary cloths. Private places for washing menstruation cloths can also be useful for women or girls to wash soiled underwear or clothing.

4. Women should be asked about what would be appropriate in terms of facilities for washing and drying their cloths. Possible options include constructing separate 'menstruation' or 'hygiene' units in a few reasonably private locations, or constructing units within existing latrine and bathroom screened-unit blocks. Privacy is a key issue here as women may not want others to know when they are menstruating.

5. If units for washing and drying sanitary cloths are to be constructed, make sure that the run-off water, which will be bloody, cannot be seen (i.e. bury the waste pipe under the ground into a soak pit) and also make sure that the drying lines cannot be seen from outside the unit.

6. If sanitary cloth is to be provided in hygiene kits make sure that it is a dark colour and not white. If it is white, the blood will leave dark stains and this will make the embarrassment of drying the cloths even more difficult.

As menstruation is a little talked-about subject in many cultures, some staff may be embarrassed or feel uncomfortable about using the term 'menstruation unit' and hence an alternative term such as 'hygiene unit' could be developed which would be more culturally appropriate (see Section 7.6).

Privacy and security in relation to using excreta disposal facilities is a key issue (see Box 3.1). Women's safety may be compromised if toilets are too far from their dwellings and they may not use them if they think they are not safe. Night lighting may be provided to avoid this problem, although this is rarely possible. Sexual harassment often increases in the confines of a camp or in an emergency situation and the location of sanitation facilities should ensure that the risks to women are minimized.

Disability considerations

Disasters and armed conflict are major causes of disability. Millions of children are killed by armed conflict, but three times as many are seriously injured or permanently disabled whether from amputations, head injuries, untreated stress or other trauma. In some emergency situations, as many as 20% of the affected population may be disabled. Disasters not only create disability, but destroy the existing infrastructure and services that were meeting their needs.

Box 3.1.

Privacy and security for women

Privacy and security are vital if people are going to use latrines. In Albanian refugee centres women were forced to go to the toilet in pairs because the toilets had no locks on the doors.

Due to a lack of appropriate latrines in IDP camps in northern Uganda women and girls have been sexually assaulted and even killed when going into the bush to defecate at night. Children, both boys and girls, have also been abducted by rebels in similar situations.

Access to sanitation for people with physical impairments is often extremely difficult in emergency situations. Most excreta disposal facilities provided in emergencies are inaccessible for physically disabled people, this may force them into unhygienic practices such as open defecation and lack of handwashing and, consequently, their health is often at increased risk (Jones et al., 2002). Families struggling for their survival are often too busy to consider the needs and health of disabled members. Consultation with disabled people and their families is an essential part of the assessment and programme design process.

Unless there are no disabled people within an affected community, excreta disposal facilities should be designed to cater for their specific needs. Requirements will depend on the nature and extent of impairments and it is important that people with disabilities are consulted to determine individual practices and needs. In general, the following aspects of design and operation should be considered:

- ensure easy access to latrines by locating them closer to households with disabled people, where possible avoiding steps, steep inclines and slippery surfaces, and providing handrails;

- provide bigger cubicles for physically disabled people and construct handrails and raised pedestals where necessary;

- ensure door handles and locks are not situated so high that people with limited reach – and children – cannot use them;
- provide easily accessible handwashing facilities that are simple to operate and provide support to facilitate handwashing if required;
- raise awareness among staff and family members to avoid overprotection, pity, teasing or rejection, and to ensure that appropriate support is provided.

Many features that improve accessibility and usage for disabled people also benefit elderly people, pregnant women, young children and people who are sick, including those living with HIV/AIDS. Section 7.6 illustrates some practical measures that can be taken to design appropriate super-structure facilities for disabled people.

More detailed information on practical options can be found in Jones and Reed (2005) *Water and Sanitation for Disabled People and Other Vulnerable Groups: Designing services to increase accessibility*. WEDC, Loughborough University: UK.

Considering HIV/AIDS

HIV/AIDS also has special relevance to excreta disposal in emergencies because people living with HIV/AIDS are more vulnerable to diarrhoeal and faeco-oral diseases due to their impaired immune systems. The Inter-Agency Standing Committee Task Force on HIV/AIDS in Emergency Settings (IASC, 2003) describes a number of key actions related to excreta disposal and people living with HIV/AIDS. Some of these key actions include:

- Provide hygiene education for family and caregivers with clear instructions on how to wash and where to dispose of waste when providing care to chronically ill persons.
- Consider the appropriate placement of latrines and waterpoints to minimize girls' and women's risk of sexual violence en route.
- Help to dispel myths about contamination of water with HIV, thereby reducing discrimination against people living with or affected by HIV/AIDS.
- Facilitate access to sanitation for families with chronically ill family members; people living with HIV/AIDS may have difficulty accessing

services due to stigmatization and discrimination – and limited energy to walk long distances or wait in queues. Options such as improved bedpans may be used for chronically ill people where latrines are too far away from houses.

- Include appropriate sanitation facilities in health centres and education sites, and provide hygiene education in emergency education programmes.

- Make extra efforts to ensure that the voices of people living with HIV/AIDS are heard either directly or indirectly by representation; infected people and their families can be inadvertently or intentionally excluded from community-based decision-making.

CAFOD has developed an approach to analysing the interconnectedness of emergencies and HIV/AIDS (see Appendix 2). This analysis suggests a set of key questions that can be asked by practitioners working in sectors such as water supply and sanitation, to ensure that activities are planned and carried out with an awareness of HIV/AIDS. Direct consultation with people living with HIV/AIDS is an essential part of this process.

Children's and infants' excreta
Children's faeces are generally more infectious than those of adults since the level of excreta-related infection among children is frequently higher, children's immune systems take several years to develop, and many young children are unable to control their defecation. Consequently, pre-venting indiscriminate defecation by children is a high priority in many emergency situations. Some key points related to children's and infants' excreta are outlined below:

- The implications for proper disposal of excreta are immense: diarrhoea, which is spread easily in an environment of poor hygiene and inadequate sanitation, kills about 2.2 million people each year, most of them children under five.

- Children under five often make up a significant proportion of the population in many poorer countries – up to 20% in some instances, and this may be considerably higher in some emergencies.

- People often feel that sanitation facilities are not appropriate for children, or that children's faeces are not harmful.

- Children are both the main sufferers from excreta-related diseases and also the main excreters of the pathogens that cause diarrhoea (UNHCR, 2000). Special measures must be taken to ensure the safe disposal of children's and infants' excreta – and to provide adequate and specialized facilities for children.

- This issue must be discussed with mothers especially to identify whether nappies, potties or specially designed latrines will be necessary. The unsafe disposal of child stools, and failure to wash hands with soap (or ash) after coming into contact with stools, are probably the main practices which allow microbes into the environment of the vulnerable child.

Depending on the age of the child, the principal defecation sites for young children are in potties, appropriately designed toilets, nappies, and on the ground in or near homes.

To ensure the proper use of latrines by children, they must be made safe for children and must be usable at night (which may entail the provision of lighting and guards). While in emergency events it may not be possible to incorporate many aspects of child-friendly designs into latrines, it is nevertheless important to plan facilities taking into account certain considerations, such as smaller latrines and squat holes, so that the greatest uptake by children is encouraged. A number of different response options are summarized in Box 3.2.

Even if it was the case before the emergency, children should be discouraged from defecating directly on the ground due to the potential public health risks which could be encountered due to high numbers of children often in a relatively small area in camps. This should be particularly communicated with parents of children who are mobile (generally children older than 12 months of age) as greater mobility allows children to get out of view of the parents more quickly and they may be able to defecate without their parents' awareness. In such instances it is important to monitor toddlers and make sure that stools are disposed of adequately.

Box 3.2.

Excreta disposal solutions for infants and children

In Rwanda in 1994 special children's latrines were provided in IDP camps and used by children aged two and above. The latrines had smaller squat holes and were open as children were afraid of using enclosed latrines. A similar approach was used in IDP camps in Uganda in 2006 (see photograph).

In camps in Freetown, Sierra Leone in 2000, potties were distributed to all families with children under five (one potty between two children).

In Albania and Macedonia in 1999 disposable nappies were provided in some of the hygiene kits distributed to refugee families by aid agencies. Whilst they were convenient they were also difficult to dispose of and were often found to be creating an additional public health risk as they were often found littered around the camp. Washable nappies would have been preferable and mothers claimed they preferred them as it was what they were used to.

In the cyclone-affected areas of Sindh Province, Pakistan, in 1999 the normal practice was to cover infants' faeces with mud and discard them outside the house. In response, a hygiene promotion programme was launched to raise awareness of the associated health risks. It successfully persuaded mothers to bury infants' excreta further away from their dwellings.

3.4 Selecting appropriate technologies

In order to determine what excreta disposal technologies should be selected for a given situation, technical, environmental, social and managerial issues should be considered. Even during chronic emergencies, there should be a participatory approach to selecting appropriate interventions. Consultation and thorough assessment are essential to ensure that appropriate options are selected that will be accepted and used properly by the affected community.

The key criteria that should be considered are:

- cultural practices/preferences
- available space
- ground conditions
- time constraints

- design life
- availability of resources
- operation and maintenance
- financial constraints

In addition, water availability, anal-cleansing materials, menstruation, user-friendliness (e.g. for children and disabled people), political issues and logistical requirements should also be considered.

It is important that technologies are not pre-decided before adequate assessment and consultation. In some cases latrine construction might not be the most appropriate option. For example, in rural communities where people go to the bush to defecate and population densities are low, it may be perfectly acceptable to continue this practice while encouraging people to bury faeces.

The approach that should be used in selecting appropriate technologies with respect to the following chapters of this manual is outlined below:

1. Conduct a rapid assessment of technical, environmental and social factors. Consult different groups within the affected community to determine usual excreta disposal practice.

2. Determine whether it is possible to implement the technology/ practice that the population is accustomed to in the current environment and in the required time-frame.

3. If action is required immediately (i.e. within hours or days) select the 1st phase option which is closest to current practice and begin community mobilization* (**Chapter 4**).

4. Determine whether the existing environmental conditions are creating an especially difficult situation (e.g. high water-table, difficulty in excavation, flooding, crowded urban areas).

5. If it is not a difficult situation select the 2nd phase option which is closest to current practice and begin community mobilization* (**Chapter 5**).

6. Otherwise, select an option for difficult situations which is closest to current practice and begin community mobilization* (**Chapter 6**).

7. Determine whether family, shared or communal latrines should be constructed (**use Table 3.3**).

8. Determine design specifications and select construction materials (**Chapter 7**).

* Community mobilization refers here to hygiene promotion activities to encourage appropriate use of selected technologies. This process should also involve consultation to ensure that alternative suggestions from community members are considered and that they are in agreement with the selected option.

Note: Options for implementation in the 1st and 2nd phases of an emergency are presented in Chapters 4 and 5 respectively. Alternative options for difficult situations are presented in Chapter 6.

A simplified technology-selection process for excreta disposal is summarized on page 44.

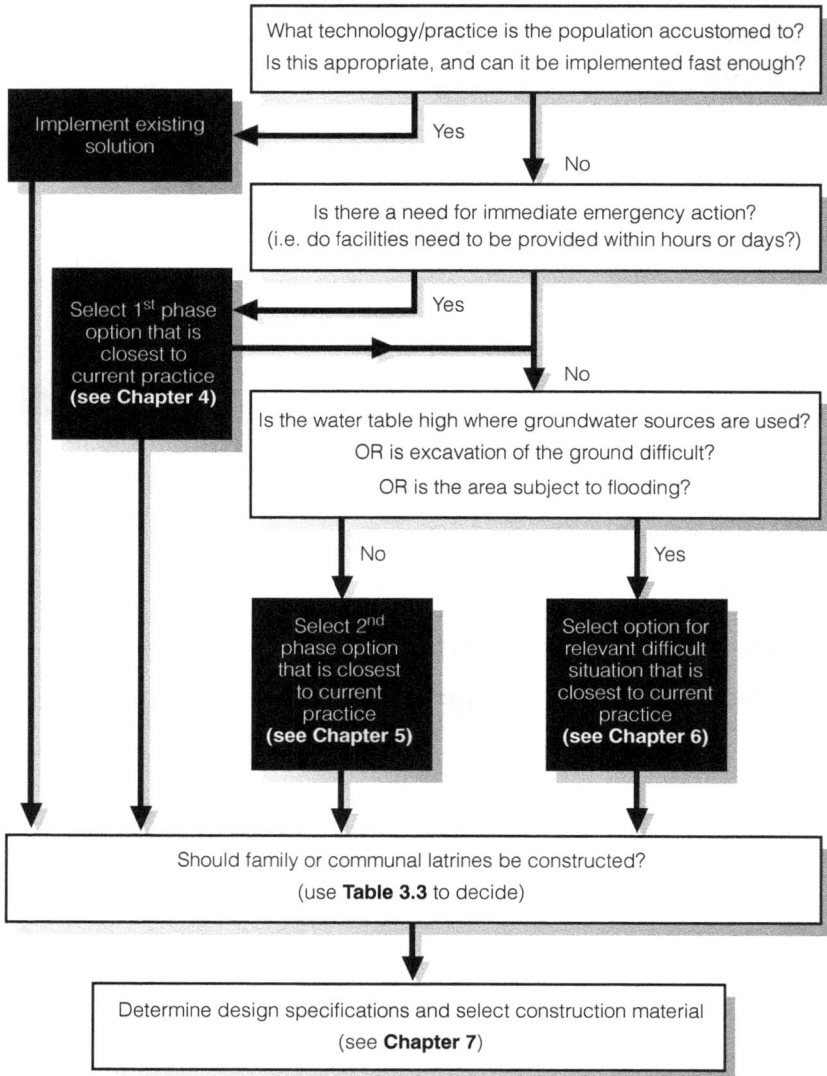

Figure 3.1. Technology selection process for excreta disposal

3.5 Implementation

Emergency implementation is rapidly transforming a planned programme into reality in the field. To ensure that implementation runs smoothly and quickly it is first necessary to have a properly thought-out plan, or programme design. Once the planning has been done, implementation is simply a question of managing the various programme components as efficiently and effectively as possible.

The primary goal of any excreta disposal programme is to:

Improve and sustain the health and well-being of the affected population.

Such a goal is crucial and should be kept in mind at all times during implementation. All activities should be geared towards this ultimate goal. Implementation targets are simply a means to an end and should always be viewed as such.

The term 'implementation' should not apply solely to the practical implementation of activities outlined in the detailed programme design. It should also apply to the day-to-day planning of those activities and how they are to be managed or co-ordinated. It also includes how contingencies are to be planned for and managed, and how the programme is to be monitored.

Implementation involves managing, planning for, and monitoring the seven key components indicated below. These components can then be used to form frameworks for implementation and monitoring.

- **Staff** – ensure fair recruitment and remuneration; look for existing professionals among the affected population; provide job descriptions, appropriate training, supervision, and security.

- **Resources** – use locally available materials and tools wherever possible, to stimulate and contribute to the local economy and to avoid extensive delays caused by ordering, purchase and transportation of resources from international sources.

- **Finances** – in preparing budgets, generous margins should be made to allow for contingency plans, operation and maintenance costs; in most situations it is best to budget for the long-term, as it is likely to be easier to secure funds in the earlier stages of an emergency.

- **Time** – ensure time is managed effectively and that activities are prioritized; break down activities into short, distinct time-bound targets; allow realistic time-frames for logistical procedures and training needs.

- **Outputs** – completed facilities or services, effective operation and maintenance systems and improvements in hygiene practice must be constantly monitored to assess progress and priorities.

- **Community** – community members should be involved in programme development and in various areas of implementation (i.e. not just by providing construction labour); ways in which to promote and sustain the capacity and self-sufficiency of the affected community must be sought continually.

- **Information** – develop an information-flow system that runs through the technical team, hygiene promotion team, logistics and finance; develop reporting formats, schedules and a regular meeting plan with the team and other key stakeholders.

Programme management

A common problem affecting emergency-relief programmes is ineffective management of the components listed above. Programme management can be defined as the planning, organization, monitoring and control of all implementation components. This must, however, be coupled with motivating all those involved in a programme to achieve its objectives. The management and co-ordination of activities is necessary to:

- achieve the programme objectives and targets;

- take immediate corrective actions for problems encountered;

- promote better communication among technical and hygiene staff in order to harmonize resources and activities for the achievement of project objectives; and

- establish communication between the affected population and other stakeholders.

The programme co-ordinator or manager is responsible for ensuring that these aims are met. The key roles of any manager are to:

- plan;

- lead;

- organize;
- control; and
- motivate.

Management can involve any or all of the following:

- self-management
- recruitment and training
- motivation and supervision
- contract negotiation
- conflict resolution
- information and record keeping
- communication and report writing
- financial management

This is not an exhaustive list; a good manager should, however, be adept at each of these and adopt a management style suitable for the current situation. For example, in the immediate stage of an emergency it may be appropriate to adopt a directive management style, whereby decisions are made rapidly with minimum input from subordinates. It is unlikely that such an approach would be appropriate in later stages of the programme, however, where a more consultative style may be more effective. Therefore, a flexible management style is likely to be necessary.

Managing implementation

A simple way to manage programme implementation is to use implementation milestones. This technique can be used with a multidisciplinary management team and usefully feeds into the monitoring process. A milestones table should be produced for each intended project output in the logical framework. Each table lists time-bound specific targets or 'milestones' which are necessary to achieve the project output. The table also includes who is responsible for achieving each milestone and when they should be completed. The final column is to be used by the management team to monitor programme progress, identify any problems or constraints, and make changes to implementation plans and time-frames.

Table 3.5 shows the typical framework for a milestones table with examples of the type of milestone and responsible bodies that may be included.

Table 3.5. Implementation by milestones

Selected milestones (general examples)	Who	When (date)	Current status
Recruitment	Agency staff		
Training of staff	Agency staff		
Resource procurement	Logistics team		
Construction of latrines	Construction team; Community		
Hygiene promotion activities	Hygiene promotion team; Community		
Monitoring activities	Agency staff; Community; Other agencies		

Contingency planning

Due to the unpredictability of many emergency situations, a key aspect of managing an emergency programme is the ability to undertake contingency planning for unforeseen events. In any emergency situation, it is difficult to plan for everything and impossible to predict exactly what will happen during the implementation phase. It is worth considering what assumptions have been made during programme design, and what is likely to happen if these assumptions prove to be wrong.

Whilst it is not necessary to make detailed contingency plans, it is good practice to consider possible emergency situations such as an influx of a large number of refugees, an outbreak of cholera or an increased security threat. Contingency plans may include:

- **Training**: appropriate training of staff in contingency procedures
- **Equipment**: local storage of small stocks of equipment in case of emergency

- **Sites**: identification of possible sites for relocation/settlement of refugees
- **Logistics**: identification of most efficient transport types and access routes

Co-ordination

One common problem in sanitation programmes is the lack of communication and collaboration between technical staff and hygiene promotion staff. This is largely a result of the fact that personnel with different professional backgrounds and interests are usually employed for each. Hygiene promotion activities are an essential part of any sanitation programme and hence all activities should be integrated from the onset of implementation. Orientation for the whole team is important to highlight the shared objectives. Joint work planning, co-ordination of field visits (including transport), and regular information-sharing meetings are key factors in achieving this aim.

It is also essential that there are good communication links between the affected community and other stakeholders, in order to avoid conflict and promote co-operation. These links should be co-ordinated by the programme manager.

The manager may also be responsible for co-ordination with other programmes and agencies working in the programme area. Ideally, different activities within the same agency should be integrated, and co-operation or collaboration with other agencies should be encouraged where possible. Integrated programmes may include sanitation, hygiene promotion, water supply, food distribution and health care activities.

Agencies can also work together in the form of water and sanitation clusters to agree on common goals and co-ordinated, consistent strategies. Such working groups can also work together to develop appropriate guidelines for a particular emergency situation. An example from Pakistan is presented in Appendix 3.

4.

1st Phase Technical Options

This chapter presents a range of technical options for 1st phase emergency implementation. It should be used to identify possible solutions for a specific situation. The final choice of option should be decided upon only after CONSULTATION with the intended users.

4.1 Immediate action

Once the outline programme design or rough action plan has been produced, immediate actions should be implemented to stabilize the current situation and prevent rapid deterioration as a result of disease transmission. A range of technical options for immediate action in the 1st phase of an emergency are presented in this chapter.

The priority for 1st Phase options is, undoubtedly, speed of implementation. It is essential that technologies to contain excreta can be installed rapidly. Options may have limited socio-cultural acceptability due to the need for speed but, wherever possible, members of the affected community should be consulted regarding the distribution and type of facilities to be implemented. Efforts should be made to separate facilities by sex and to address any major cultural practices or beliefs relating to excreta disposal. If this is not done there is a real danger that facilities will not be used at all.

Selected options are likely to have limited sustainability, since they are designed for use in the immediate emergency phase only. It is important, however, that likely, future excreta disposal options are considered at this stage to ensure that immediate measures do not have a detrimental effect on longer-term solutions.

4.2 Managing open defecation

In the initial stages of an emergency, areas where people can defecate, rather than where they cannot, should be provided immediately. If there is insufficient time to construct appropriate facilities this may mean, in extreme circumstances, the setting up of open defecation areas. These should be located where excreta cannot contaminate the food chain or water sources.

Where there is a large and rapid influx of people into an area one of the immediate steps that must be taken is to prevent indiscriminate defecation (see Box 4.1). It is also likely that it will be necessary to instigate a clean-up operation where workers with wheelbarrows and lime are employed to clean the area of faeces. This must, however, be accompanied by the provision of areas where people are allowed to defecate and must be actively enforced with appropriate hygiene messages.

Box 4.1.

Preventing indiscriminate open defecation

In Tanzania during the 1994 Rwandan refugee crisis one approach adopted in the immediate emergency phase was to employ sanitation workers whose primary task was to forcibly prevent people defecating in certain areas around the refugee camp – and to direct them to alternative areas or facilities. This was especially important on the lakeside of the camp to prevent faecal contamination entering the lake which was the main water source, and was accompanied by a clean-up operation and the provision of open defecation areas.

Such an approach had to be managed carefully to avoid conflict within the affected population and was accompanied by appropriate hygiene promotion, highlighting the need to prevent water contamination at the earliest possible stage.

In some emergency situations it may be perfectly acceptable for the affected population to practice open defecation. Indeed, in some cultures defecating in the open is preferred to using a latrine. Where people are accustomed to open defecation it may be appropriate to continue this, providing there is adequate space and vegetation to allow people to find an appropriate defecation space so that the risk of disease transmission is minimized. People should, however, be encouraged to use the 'cat' method whereby a shallow indent is made and faeces are covered with soil.

WHEREVER POSSIBLE AVOID DEFECATION FIELDS

AND INSTALL TRENCH LATRINES AS A FIRST OPTION

Where there is insufficient time to provide facilities for a disaster-affected population, open defecation areas should be used only as an extreme short-term measure before latrines are ready for use. Defecation areas or fields surrounded by screening may be set up, with segregated sites for each sex. People should be encouraged to use one strip of land at a time and used areas must be clearly marked. It is also possible to use internal partitions to provide more privacy and encourage greater use.

It is essential that defecation areas are:

- far from water storage and treatment facilities;
- at least 50m from water sources;
- downhill of settlements and water sources;
- far from public buildings or roads;
- not in field crops grown for human consumption;
- far from food storage or preparation areas.

Advantages: Rapid to implement; minimal resources required; minimizes indiscriminate open defecation.

Constraints: Lack of privacy for users; considerable space required; difficult to manage; considerable potential for cross-contamination of users; better suited to hot, dry climates.

In extreme situations it may be necessary to make temporary open defecation fields by just marking off areas with tape. However, this is rarely necessary and the lack of privacy may make them ineffective. It is nearly always possible to at least surround an area in plastic sheeting or fabric and dig a few shallow trenches.

Whilst simple in concept and construction, the operation of defecation fields requires careful control to ensure they are used as intended to keep health risks to a minimum. Attendants will need to be recruited and provided with training to encourage effective use of the trenches and to encourage handwashing following use. A network of public health promoters will also be needed to sensitize the population on the importance of using the fields. It is rare that these fields will be used by everyone, as privacy will be a major issue and, therefore, they should only be instigated if the risks are significant and if there is no other rapidly implemented alternative.

Location of defecation fields

The location of the field must be discussed with the population. The field should be at least 30 metres from dwellings but located as centrally as possible to the people who are going to use them (within 100 metres of shelters if possible). They should be on land sloping away from the camp and surface water sources, the field should be surrounded by a drain so that surface water cannot enter and to prevent any runoff from the field contaminating other areas. Whilst an open field is easier to manage, the affected population may prefer a site with trees, and bushes to provide privacy. Consideration should be given to the direction of prevailing winds, to reduce the nuisance caused by odour. Areas subject to flooding or containing running water should be avoided. The soil should be easy to dig so that faeces can be buried. The defecation field should be provided with adequate surface drains to prevent surface water running across them from above – and to collect and contain any seepage of liquid effluent.

Operation of defecation fields

Users need to be encouraged to use the strips furthest away from the entrance; to cover their own excreta with earth; and to wash their hands afterwards. To ensure the sanitary use of the field:

- provide full-time supervision in the form of paid attendants;

- provide anal-cleansing materials and methods for their safe disposal; and

- provide handwashing facilities.

Each field should have at least two people present at all times to guide the individual to the right area and ensure that other areas of the field are not used. Marking tape and paint can be used to mark out the zones, make signs to direct people to the correct area for defecation and post other simple messages on any suitable board or surface. A 200l plastic barrel with fitted tap can be situated at the entrance of the area for hand-washing. Soap or ash should also be provided for effective handwashing. If neither is available, the barrel can be filled with a 0.05% chlorine solution. A 0.05% solution is made by adding half a tablespoon (7.5g) of High Test Hypochlorite HTH (70% active chlorine) granules, or 15g of bleaching powder (approx. 35% active chlorine), to 10l of water. It may be necessary to provide extra handwashing facilities depending on the numbers of people using the field. (See Chapter 8 for details of handwashing options.) All excreta should be covered with soil as soon as possible to prevent the breeding of flies and reduce odours. If the users do not cover their faeces then the attendants should.

Where water is used for anal-cleansing, a container of water should be supplied at the entrance to the field, together with small pots for individual use. This can be managed by the attendants along with the handwashing facilities. Where solids are used, the appropriate material may also need to be provided along with receptacles to collect soiled material. These materials should then be buried or burned and not deposited where they will create a health hazard.

4.3 Shallow trench latrines

A simple improvement on open defecation fields is to provide shallow trenches in which people can defecate. This allows users to cover faeces and improves the overall hygiene and convenience of an open defecation system. Trenches need only be 200-300mm wide and 150mm deep, and shovels may be provided to allow each user to cover their excreta with soil.

Divide the field into strips 1.5m wide with access paths. Use strips furthest from the entrance first. When a section of trench has its bottom layer fully covered with excreta it is filled in. Only short lengths of trench should be opened for use at any one time to encourage the full utilization of the trench in a short time. It may be appropriate to have a number of trenches open at the same time. A rule of thumb is to allow 0.25m^2 of land per person per day. This means 2,500m^2 per 10,000 people per day, or nearly two hectares per week. Men's and women's areas should always be separated.

Where possible make the plastic sheeting or bamboo-mat walls higher than a standing person to ensure complete privacy.

Advantages: Rapid to implement (one worker can dig 50m of trench per day); faeces can be covered easily with soil.

Constraints: Limited privacy; short life-span; considerable space required.

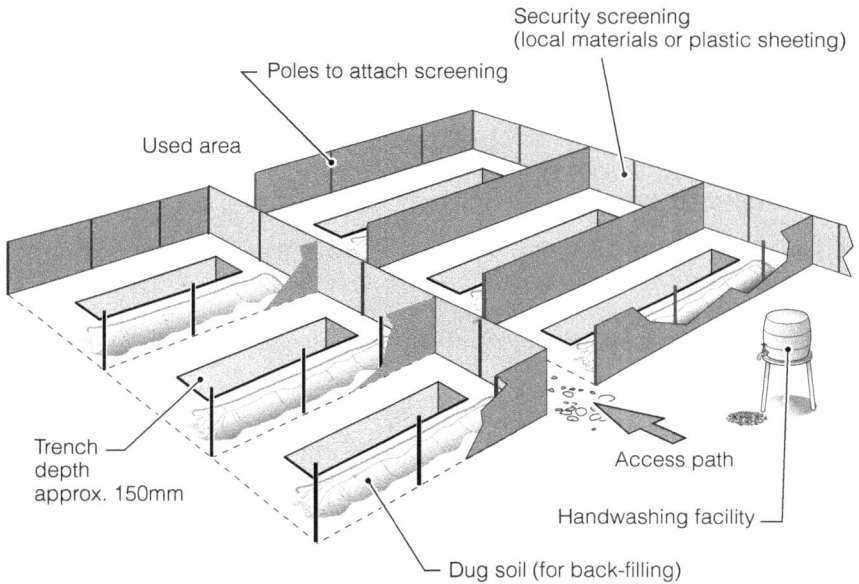

Superstructure

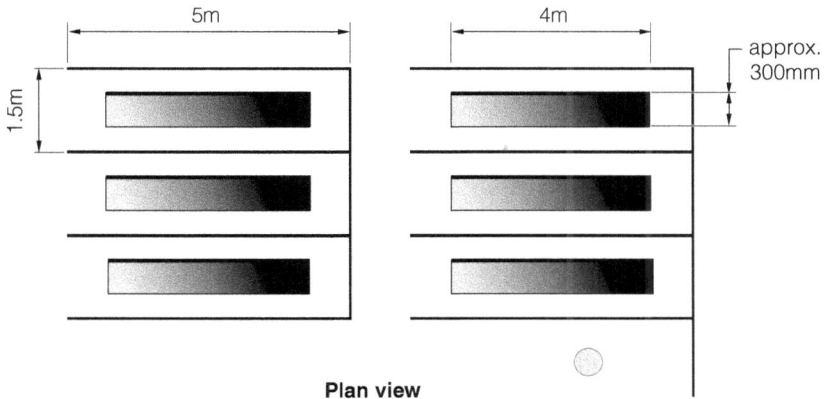

5m 4m approx. 300mm

1.5m

Plan view

Figure 4.1. Shallow trench latrines

4.4 Deep trench latrines

Deep trench latrines are often constructed in the immediate stage of an emergency and will be appropriate if there are sufficient tools, materials and human resources available. These involve the siting of several cubicles above a single trench which is used to collect the excreta. However, care should be taken not to provide too many latrines side by side. The recommended **maximum** length of trench is 6m, providing **six cubicles**.

Trenches should be 0.8-0.9m wide and **at least the top 0.5m of the pit should be lined** to ensure that the trench remains stable. There are a number of different pit-lining materials that can be used including concrete, bricks, blocks, sandbags, and timber (see Section 7.3).

After the trench has been dug, the quickest option is to put self-supporting plastic slabs straight over the trench. If slabs are not available, then wooden planks can be secured across the trench until proper wooden or concrete slabs can be made (see Section 7.4). The trench should be covered with planks leaving out every third or fourth plank, which is where people defecate. Planks should overlap each side of the trench by **at least 15cm**. Ideally, all designs should be discussed with the community beforehand – and should take into account the safety of women and children and elderly or disabled people.

The latrine superstructure can be made from local materials, such as grass matting, cloth or wood, or plastic sheeting (though this often makes the interior very hot). The emphasis should be on using materials which are readily available and that can be applied rapidly. Some agencies have rapid-response kits for slabs and superstructures which can be used where there are few resources locally. Section 7.6 contains information on superstructure options.

Advantages: Cheap; quick to construct; no water needed for operation; easily understood.

Constraints: Unsuitable where water-table is high, soil is too unstable to dig or ground is very rocky; often odour problems; cleaning and maintenance of communal trench latrines are often poorly carried out by users.

See **Appendix 4.1** for a bill of quantities for a deep trench latrine.

Partitions of local materials 1m apart

Timber foot rests and floor plates

Lightweight timber frame

Excavated soil
(used for back-fill)

Plastic
sheeting
door flap

Partition wall

Plastic sheeting

Spacing of foot rests
varied to suit adults and
children (no more than 150mm apart)

Trench 0.8m wide
x 2.0m deep, length
to suit the number
of cubicles required

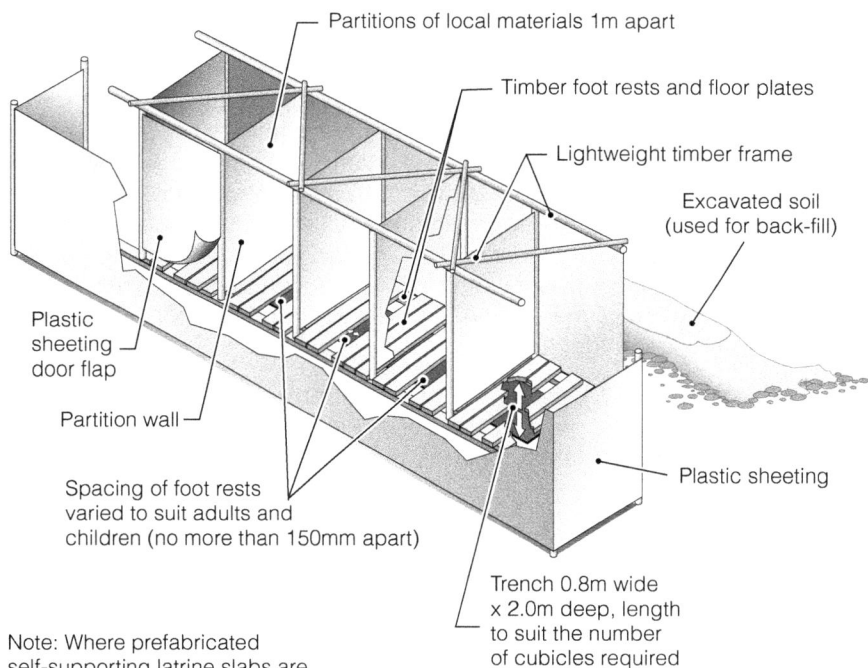

Note: Where prefabricated
self-supporting latrine slabs are
to be used in place of timber
cubicle sizes may need to be
adjusted to fit slab width
(e.g. 0.8m)

Superstructure

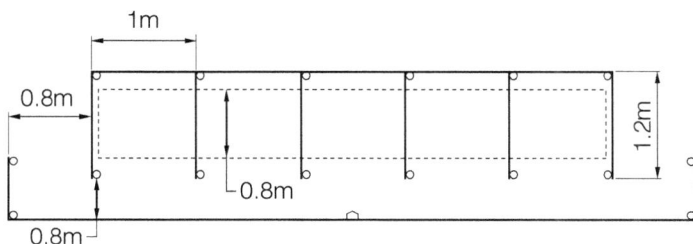

1m

0.8m

0.8m

1.2m

0.8m

Plan view

Figure 4.2. Deep trench latrines

59

4.5 Shallow family latrines

In some emergency situations it may be more appropriate to provide shallow family (rather than trench) latrines. This is particularly suitable where people are keen to build their own latrines, or have experience of latrine construction and, where there is sufficient space, but where rocky soil or high water-tables makes deeper excavation difficult. A shallow pit of approximately 0.3m x 0.5m x 0.5m depth may be excavated. Wooden foot-rests or a latrine slab (approximately 0.8m x 0.6m) can be placed over this, overlapping by at least 15cm on each side. This latrine should be an immediate measure only and back-filling should occur when the pit is full to within 0.2m of the slab. A simple superstructure for privacy can be made from local materials.

Conventional family pit latrines will be the preferred option in most cases (see Section 5.1) but, where time and environmental conditions do not allow this, shallow family latrines provide an immediate short-term option.

Advantages: Increased privacy; rapid to implement; reduced labour input from agency; allow people to actively participate in finding an appropriate solution.

Constraints: Community must be willing and able to construct family latrines; difficult to manage siting and back-filling of pits; large quantity of tools and materials required.

Privacy screen of local materials or plastic sheeting

Height approx. 1.5m

Entrance

Wooden foot rests

Hole approx. 300mm x 500mm x 500mm deep, (will need to be smaller for young children)

300mm

150mm

Privacy screen

500mm

400mm

Wooden foot rests

Entrance

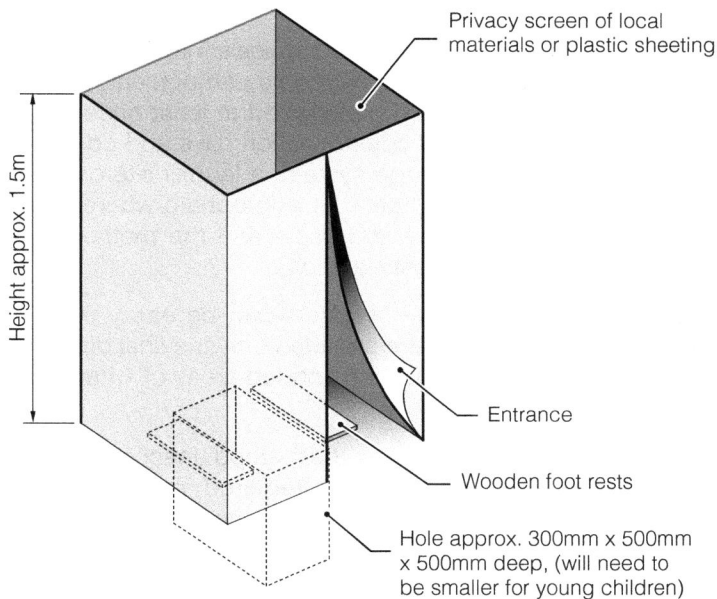

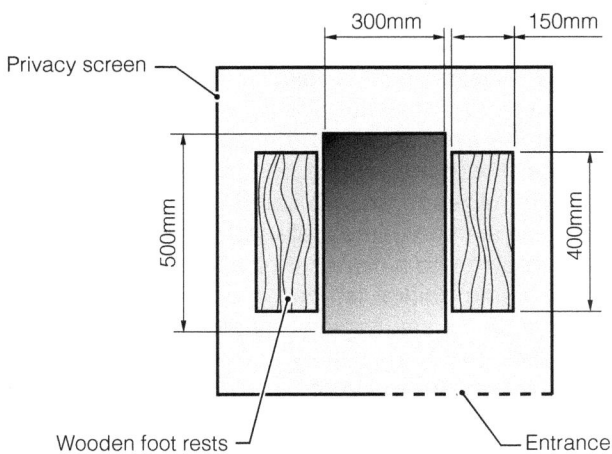

Plan view of latrine

Figure 4.3. Shallow family latrines

4.6 Bucket latrines

In situations where there is limited space it may be appropriate to provide buckets or containers in which people can defecate. These should have tight-fitting lids and should be emptied at least once a day. Disinfectant may be added to reduce contamination risks and odour. Containers can be emptied into a sewerage system, a landfill site or waste-stabilization ponds. This measure will only be appropriate where there are no other immediate action options and users find the method acceptable; it is, therefore, not used in most situations.

Advantages: Defecation containers can be easily procured and transported; once containers are provided only the final disposal system need be constructed; can be used in flooded areas or where the water-table is very high.

Constraints: Many people find the method unacceptable; large quantities of containers and disinfectant are required; extensive education regarding final disposal is required; disposal site must be fairly close to homes to minimize transportation needs; containers may be used for alternative purposes.

4.7 Packet latrines

In some emergency situations relief agencies have provided disposable packet latrines. These are plastic packets (similar in appearance to a plastic bag) in which the user can defecate; the packets contain a blend of enzymes which assists the breakdown of the excreta, and must be disposed of in a safe place. There are various commercial options available containing different chemicals to absorb liquids, aid organic decay and neutralize odours. These are sometimes referred to as 'flying' latrines since the packets can be thrown into a disposal pit or container. Effective management of a system using packet latrines is crucial, and requires ongoing monitoring and appropriate hygiene promotion. Appropriate disposal sites must be developed immediately and an active campaign initiated to inform community members. Basic consultation with the community is necessary before implementing such a system.

Advantages: Lightweight and easy to transport; may be used where space is severely limited or in flooded areas.

Constraints: Method may not be acceptable to affected population; final disposal site must be clearly marked, accessible and used.

4.8 Chemical toilets

Chemical toilets (known as 'porta-loos') are portable sanitation units that consist of a sit-down toilet (e.g. in South America) or a squatting pan (e.g. in South Asia) placed above a water-tight excreta-holding tank, which usually contains a chemical solution to aid digestion and reduce odour. This is contained in a single prefabricated plastic unit with a lockable door. They range in quality from very basic units to luxury units which come complete with warm-water handwashing facilities.

Chemical toilets have been adopted as temporary solutions where pit latrines or septic-tanks are unsuitable or unacceptable. The initial charge of chemical is adequate for 40 to 160 uses, depending upon the model. Floors are typically made from non-absorbent material, and the finish is easily cleanable. There is often a means of ventilation through a screened pipe which extends above the roofline.

There are several considerations that should be taken into account when implementing this solution. The siting of the toilets is important as they must be serviced and desludged regularly to prevent overflow. This means that the toilets must be located in an area that can be accessible to a big truck. However, another important consideration is that because of their strong smell, especially when they are being cleaned, it may not be preferable to locate them close to public thoroughfares or close to areas where people are living. The toilets must also be positioned on a very flat surface to avoid them tipping over. An example of their application is described in Box 4.2.

Advantages: Portable; hygienic; minimized odour; can be mobilized rapidly.

Constraints: High cost; difficult to transport; unsustainable; regular servicing and emptying required; uncommon outside Europe, North America and parts of Latin America.

Box 4.2.

Chemical toilets deployed in flood response in the Dominican Republic

The use of chemical toilets was chosen as the first-phase excreta disposal option in flood response in the Dominican Republic in 2003, as they were mobile and could be quickly deployed once local suppliers were identified. The toilets arrived approximately two days after people arrived in the shelters and supplemented latrines already at these sites. Chemical toilets at displaced centres were a rapid and effective solution, as was the initial period of installation in the communities where all latrines were either flooded or destroyed.

In this case, two types of chemical toilets were used – one which had a separate urinal for men and one with a box seat. In these particular toilets, prior to use the excreta-holding tank is charged with a mixture of water (between 30 and 100 litres) and chemical concentrate. The chemical is a solution of sodium hydroxide or another approved chemical. Its purpose is to disinfect, to neutralize offensive odours and to convert waste into sludge that can be deposited into a sewer without any adverse effects.

The chemical toilets were cleaned every other day and were used for longer than originally planned because the second-phase intervention (the construction of twin-pit dry latrines) had taken longer to implement than originally planned.

Lessons Learned: Various problems were encountered – a main disadvantage was that the use of the toilets ended up being a relatively expensive solution, especially when the use lasted longer than originally expected. Siting was also an issue as the latrines needed to be in a location that was accessible to the cleaning/ desludging truck, such as near a roadway or thoroughfare.

Hygiene promotion issues included providing an adequate amount of toilet paper for all people, in order to maintain hygienic conditions. Some people were afraid that using the toilet seats would transmit disease. Other problems were related to social aspects of communal toilet use, with families not wanting to share with other cultural groups (e.g. Haitian families) and with families wanting to move the toilets into their home for their own use.

In the future, provision for damage in the contract or insurance should be taken out to cover against unexpected accidents, such as the units being vandalized and burned down in Los Solares. Insurance against theft and vandalism should be discussed with the local supplier. Also, the agency should not have left the toilets in the communities for as long as it did. The slow removal was compounded by the slow start-up of the raised compost-latrine programme and, in some cases, people preferred the chemical toilets and didn't want them to be taken away. The community should have been involved from the onset of the implementation process and beneficiaries should have been informed of how long the toilets would be used for, and the staging/phasing of excreta disposal provision in the community.

5.

2nd Phase Technical Options

This chapter presents a range of standard technical options for 2nd phase emergency implementation. It should be used to identify possible solutions for a specific situation. Solutions for more difficult environments are presented in Chapter 6. The final choice of option(s) should be decided upon only after in depth CONSULTATION with the intended users.

This chapter considers the following technical options:

- Simple pit latrines
- Ventilated improved pit (VIP) latrines
- Eco-San options
- Borehole latrines
- Pour-flush latrines
- Septic-tanks
- Aqua-privies
- Wastewater treatment systems
- Latrines for institutions (schools, clinics etc.)

The basic characteristics and design parameters for each option are presented below. Supporting technical design information can be found in Chapter 7 and detailed bills of quantities are provided in Appendix 4 where indicated.

5.1 Simple pit latrines

Simple pit latrines are by far the most common technology choice adopted in emergency situations. This is because they are simple, quick to construct and generally inexpensive.

The **pit should be as deep as possible** (and at least 2m in depth) and covered by a latrine slab. The rate at which the pit will fill will depend on the sludge accumulation rate and the infiltration rate of the soil and the required size of the pit can be estimated based on these (see Section 7.3). At least the top 1m of the pit should be lined to prevent collapse, and where the soil is suspected to be unstable the entire pit should be lined. There are a number of lining options that can be used (see Section 7.3).

The slab can be made from concrete or wood, or a prefabricated plastic slab can be used (see Section 7.4). This should be firmly supported on all sides and raised above the surrounding ground level to prevent surface water entering the pit. A squat or drop-hole is provided in the slab which allows excreta to fall directly into the pit – this can be covered with a removable lid to minimize flies and odour.

The superstructure can be made from materials available locally, such as wood, mud and grass, or can be a more permanent structure of bricks and mortar.

Advantages: Cheap; quick to construct; no water needed for operation; easily understood.

Constraints: Unsuitable where water-table is high, soil is too unstable to dig or ground is very rocky; often odour problems.

See **Appendix 4.2** for a bill of quantities for a simple pit latrine.

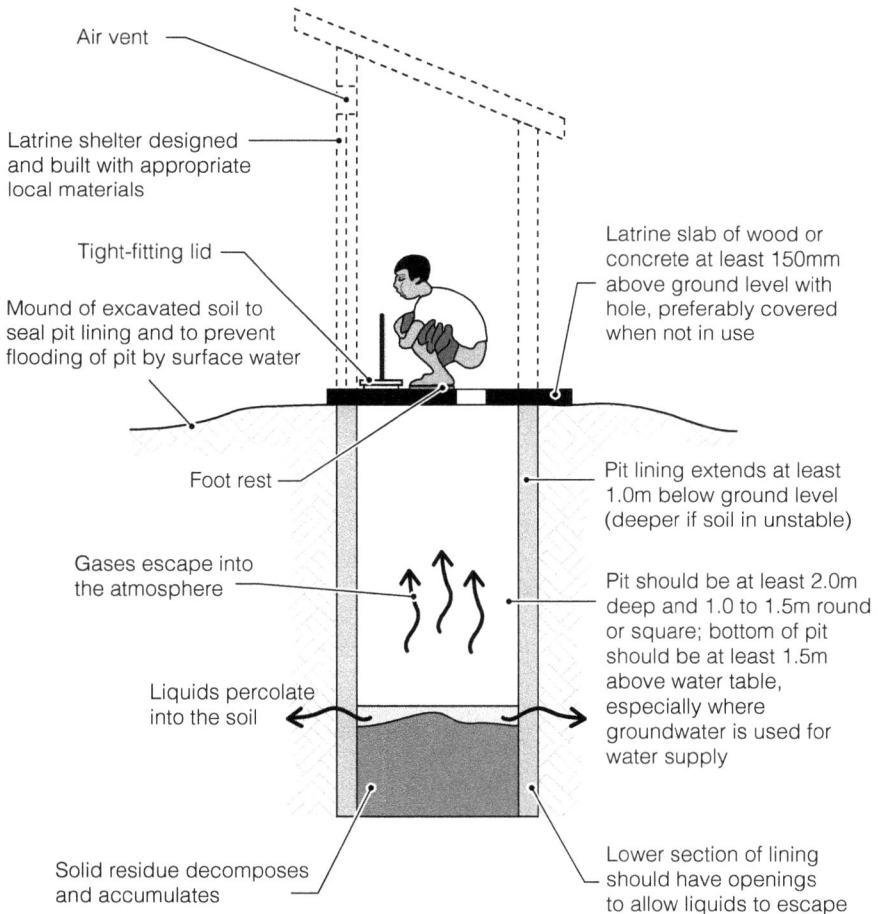

Air vent

Latrine shelter designed
and built with appropriate
local materials

Tight-fitting lid

Mound of excavated soil to
seal pit lining and to prevent
flooding of pit by surface water

Foot rest

Gases escape into
the atmosphere

Liquids percolate
into the soil

Solid residue decomposes
and accumulates

Latrine slab of wood or
concrete at least 150mm
above ground level with
hole, preferably covered
when not in use

Pit lining extends at least
1.0m below ground level
(deeper if soil in unstable)

Pit should be at least 2.0m
deep and 1.0 to 1.5m round
or square; bottom of pit
should be at least 1.5m
above water table,
especially where
groundwater is used for
water supply

Lower section of lining
should have openings
to allow liquids to escape

Figure 5.1. Simple pit latrines

5.2   Ventilated-improved pit (VIP) latrines

The Ventilated Improved Pit (VIP) latrine is an improved pit latrine designed to minimize odour and flies. This is more expensive than the simple pit latrine and, in emergency situations, is generally **only viable for institutions** such as hospitals or schools.

A **vent pipe** covered with a **gauze mesh or fly-proof netting** is incorporated into the design to remove odorous gases from the pit, prevent flies entering the pit and trap any flies trying to leave. The pipe should **extend at least 0.5m above the superstructure roof** to ensure the air flow is unobstructed, and should be at least 30cm from the squat hole. The movement of air across the top of the vent pipe creates low pressure which promotes upward air flow within the pipe and aids ventilation. The vent pipe can be situated inside or outside the latrine interior. Inside has the advantage that the latrine slab is easier to construct since the superstructure can be built around it, and outside has the advantage that the pipe warms quicker which encourages air flow through it. Air should be able to flow freely through the squat hole and vent pipe; therefore **no drop-hole cover** is required.

The superstructure interior should be kept reasonably dark to deter flies, but there should be a gap, usually above the door, to allow air to enter. This gap should be at least three times the cross-sectional area of the vent pipe (Franceys et al., 1992). Air flow can be increased by facing the door of the superstructure towards the prevailing wind. Each drop-hole should have its own compartment and there should always be **one vent pipe per compartment**.

Advantages: Reduced odour; reduces flies; good-quality. Long-term solution.

Constraints: Difficult and expensive to construct properly; design and operation often not fully understood; construction may take time; dark interior may deter young children from use; does not deter mosquitoes; low replicability as PVC pipes are expensive; increased odour outside.

See **Appendix 4.4** for a bill of quantities for a VIP latrine.

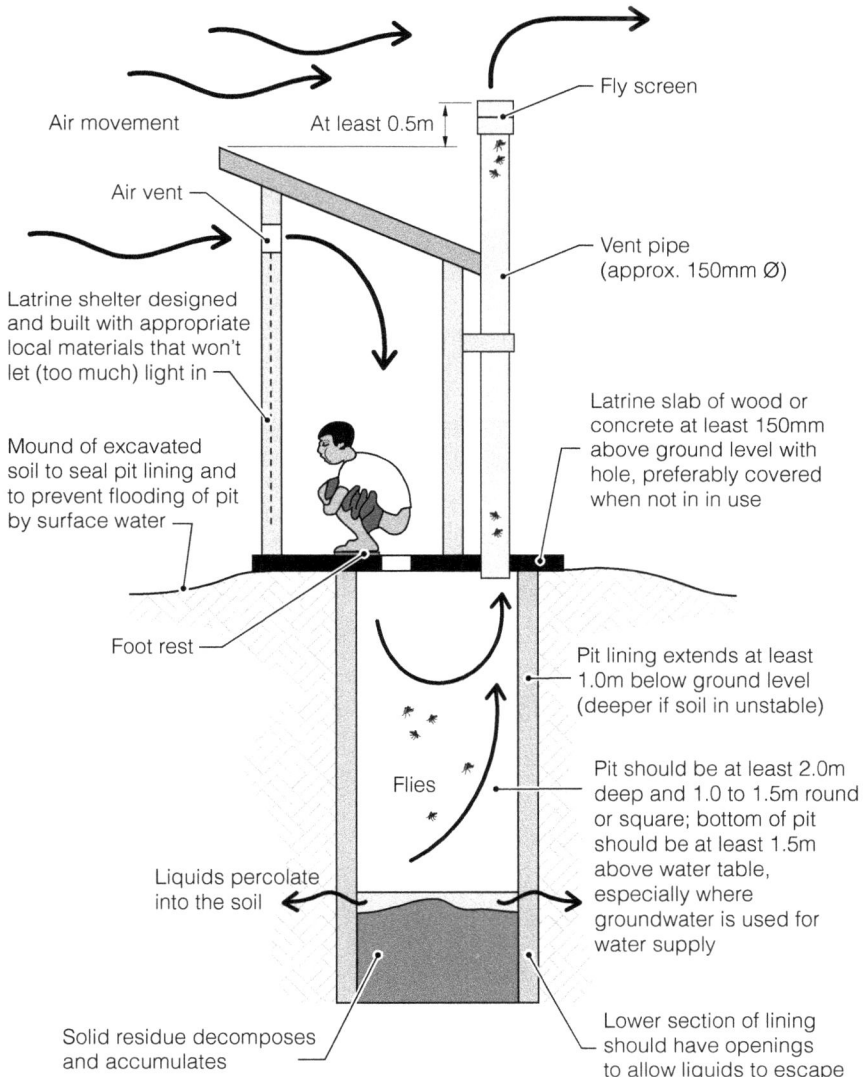

Air movement

At least 0.5m

Fly screen

Air vent

Vent pipe
(approx. 150mm Ø)

Latrine shelter designed
and built with appropriate
local materials that won't
let (too much) light in

Mound of excavated
soil to seal pit lining and
to prevent flooding of pit
by surface water

Latrine slab of wood or
concrete at least 150mm
above ground level with
hole, preferably covered
when not in in use

Foot rest

Pit lining extends at least
1.0m below ground level
(deeper if soil in unstable)

Flies

Pit should be at least 2.0m
deep and 1.0 to 1.5m round
or square; bottom of pit
should be at least 1.5m
above water table,
especially where
groundwater is used for
water supply

Liquids percolate
into the soil

Solid residue decomposes
and accumulates

Lower section of lining
should have openings
to allow liquids to escape

Figure 5.2. VIP latrines

71

Vent pipe details

The vent pipe mesh or netting should have a mesh size of between 1.2 and 1.5mm. The gases given off by the decomposition of excreta are very corrosive. For this reason, fly mesh made from mild steel will rot very quickly and plastic mesh will last about two years. Mosquito netting is often used but aluminium or stainless steel is the best material for this purpose.

A wide variety of materials can be used for the vent pipe, such as uPVC, asbestos cement, fired clay, concrete or even mud-covered bamboo or reed. If the pipe is smooth inside (such as plastic or asbestos cement) then an **internal diameter of 150mm** is recommended. The smallest PVC pipe diameter that can be used is 110mm, but only if larger diameters are not available. Otherwise vent pipes should be at least 200mm in diameter or square. Where large-diameter pipes are not available, or are too expensive, an alternative is to construct the vent pipe from block or brickwork.

A simple test can be used to check that the vent pipe is having the desired effect and that air is flowing from the pit up through the pipe. When a small amount of ignited paper and/or dry grass is dropped into the pit smoke should be seen rising from the top of the vent pipe if the ventilation effect is functioning correctly.

The majority of design and construction information for a VIP latrine, such as pit and slab design, is the same as for a simple pit latrine (see Chapter 7 for more information).

5.3 Eco-San

Ecological sanitation (or Eco-San) refers to excreta disposal solutions which recycle nutrients from human excreta for agricultural production. Eco-San options can be defined in several different ways but the most common options are the:

- **Double-vault urine-diverting latrine** which uses a dry disposal system in which urine and faeces are managed separately, and ash, carbon or sawdust is added to the vault contents; and

- **Double-vault non-urine-diverting latrine** in which urine is not separated from faeces but soil, ash and organic waste is added to the vault contents.

Both options are designed so that one vault is used initially, then sealed when full. The second vault is then used until that is full, at which point the first vault can be emptied and the stored waste re-used (for agricultural purposes). In order to make the waste safe for handling and most effective as a fertilizer, sufficient time is required to reduce the pathogen content of the waste. The vault size must be carefully calculated to ensure that the waste is retained for one to two years. Heavy usage, as is likely in many emergency situations, may lead to serious problems because of inadequate time for decomposition.

The following factors have a positive effect on reducing pathogen survival in ecological latrines (Sugden, 2006):

- increasing storage time (by using large pits or vaults);

- reducing the moisture content (ideally below 25%, by separating urine from faeces, heating, or adding wood ash or soil to absorb moisture from faeces);

- increasing the pH (ideally to above 10, by adding ash or lime – though this may have an impact on the effectiveness of the final waste product as a fertilizer);

- increasing the temperature (ideally above 36°C, by adding green organic material or using a solar-drying plate);

- encouraging the presence of other micro-organisms (by adding soil containing fungi and micro-organisms capable of predation).

Double-vault urine-diverting latrine

In the double-vault urine-diverting latrine (sometimes known as a dehydrating latrine) the deposited faecal matter is dried by exposure to heat or the sun and the addition of wood ash, carbon, sawdust or earth, which controls the moisture content. In El Salvador a 3:1 mixture of sawdust and ash or a 5:1 mixture of dry earth and lime is recommended, a handful of which should be added after each use. The latrine contents are then isolated from human contact for a specified period to reduce the presence of pathogens and make the waste safe for handling. This period should be **at least ten months** and some practitioners recommend longer periods of up to two years. The longer the waste is stored the more pathogens will be destroyed. The waste may then be re-used as fertilizer or as fuel.

The vaults can be constructed above or below ground, but above ground has the advantage that contents can be emptied more easily and there is less risk of groundwater contamination. An adaptation of the urine-diverting latrine is the solar urine-diverting latrine in which the vaults are extended at the rear of the latrine and covered with a metal plate. This is painted black and oriented to receive maximum solar insolation in order to increase the temperature of the vault contents.

The primary difficulty in using this type of toilet is the separation of urine and faeces. Users have to be made aware of the importance of separation and the addition of ash after defecation. Such a system is unlikely to work where water is used for anal-cleansing since this will increase the moisture content. In general, urine-separation latrines are not appropriate in the initial stages of an emergency, due to the time taken to educate, train and construct. However, they require no water and can be adopted where infiltration techniques are impossible – and may be a viable longer-term option.

Advantages: Reduced odour; ideal where the affected population normally uses Eco-San latrines and agricultural activity occurs; raised latrines can be used to prevent groundwater contamination.

Constraints: more difficult to construct than simple pit latrines; high level of user awareness and diligence required; complex to operate and maintain.

See **Appendix 4.5** for a bill of quantities for a double-vault urine-diverting latrine.

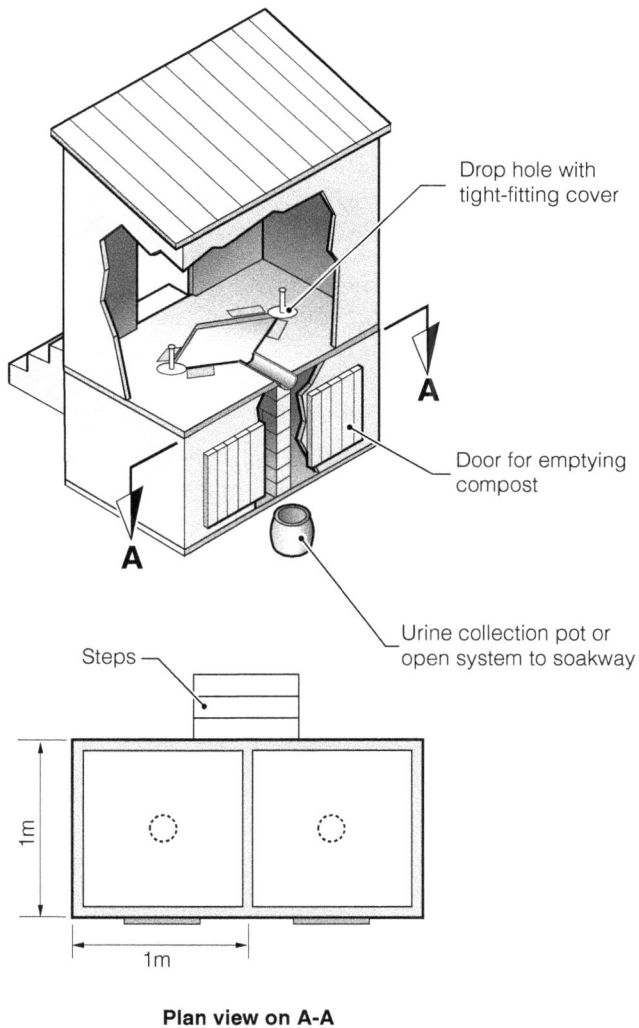

Drop hole with
tight-fitting cover

Door for emptying
compost

Urine collection pot or
open system to soakway

Steps

1m

1m

Plan view on A-A

Figure 5.3. Double-vault urine-diverting latrine

Double-vault non-urine-diverting latrine

The double-vault non-urine-diverting composting latrine (also known as the Fossa Alterna) is very similar to the urine-separation latrine. It also has two vaults or pits which are used alternately and can be constructed above or below ground level. The waste must be stored for at least one year (and preferably two years) before re-use.

The principal difference between the two latrine types is that urine is not separated from faeces which makes it easier to construct and use. In order to raise the temperature and increase the effectiveness of the waste as a fertilizer the composting process is encouraged through the addition of earth, wood ash and green organic material. A 3:1 mixture of dry earth and ash can be added after each use to raise the pH and encourage predation. Vegetable or other organic waste such as food residue can also be added to control the chemical balance. A solar heating plate can also be used to help raise the temperature.

Once the pit or vault is two-thirds full it should be topped up with earth to allow anaerobic composting to take place while the second pit is in use.

Ecological latrines are not appropriate in most emergencies. However, they may be appropriate if the population is already accustomed to using similar systems or if family latrines are to be constructed in an agricultural area. Raised latrines can also be effective in preventing contamination of shallow groundwater.

Photograph 5.1. Solar urine-diverting latrine in El Salvador

Biogas latrines

Biogas technology, whereby the gas given off by decomposing excreta is captured and used for fuel, has been promoted in some low-income countries such as China, India, Nepal, Thailand, Cambodia and Vietnam. Low-cost, plastic-tubular biodigesters can be used to digest large volumes of human or animal waste to provide gas which is used as cooking fuel. This technology may be appropriate where there is local indigenous experience and expertise in designing and managing such plants. It is not, however, appropriate for the majority of emergency situations where this expertise is not available.

5.4   Borehole latrines

Borehole latrines can be constructed very rapidly if an auger or a drilling rig is available. A deep soil profile (more than 7m) is required which is relatively easy to drill with a hand auger or a mechanical drill. The borehole has a typical diameter of 400mm and a depth of 5-10m. A hole 300mm in diameter and 5 metres deep should last a family of five approximately two years, depending on the material used for anal-cleansing. At least the top 0.5m should be lined although it is rarely necessary or appropriate to line the entire depth.

Borehole latrines are most appropriate in situations where boring/drilling equipment is readily available, where a large number of latrines must be constructed rapidly, and where pits are difficult to excavate, either because of ground conditions or the lack of a suitable labour force.

Advantages: The borehole can be excavated quickly if boring equipment is available; suitable in hard ground conditions (where there are no large stones or rocks); and appropriate where only a small workforce is available.

Constraints: Drilling equipment is required; there is a greater risk of groundwater pollution due to greater depth than pit latrines; lifespan is short; sides are liable to be fouled, causing odour and attracting flies; and there is a high likelihood of blockages.

This option should only be considered in extreme conditions when pit excavation is not possible.

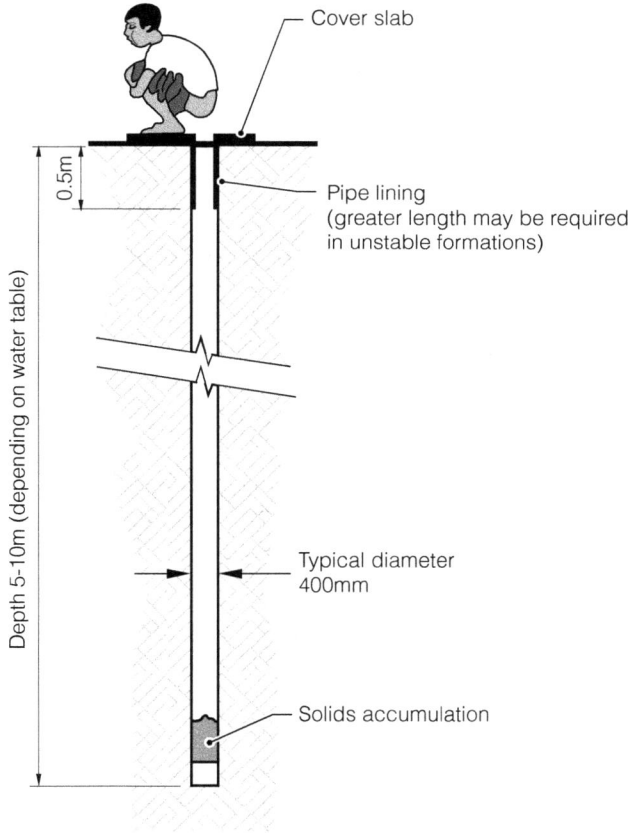

Figure 5.4. Borehole latrine

5.5 Pour-flush latrines

Pour-flush latrines rely on water to act as a hygienic seal and to help remove excreta to a wet or dry disposal system. The most simple pour-flush latrines use a latrine pan incorporating a shallow U-bend which retains the water. After defecation, a few litres of water must be poured, or thrown, into the bowl in order to flush the excreta into the pit or sewerage system below. Ideally, adequate water must be made available near to latrines. If this is not possible, people may take their own containers when using toilets.

Pour-flush latrines may be constructed directly above a pit or may be offset whereby the waste travels through a discharge pipe to a pit or septic-tank.

Even where there is limited water available, wherever possible pour-flush latrines should be implemented if the population is already accustomed to using them. This is because often such people will not be prepared to use dry systems. Consultation with the community is essential in order to determine the best option.

The amount of water required to flush the system will depend on the type and size of the water-seal construction. A 90mm (3") U-bend normally requires 2-3 litres to flush effectively, while a 120mm (4") U-bend generally requires 4-5 litres to flush. These quantities are significantly less than the amount required to flush most water-closet toilets which may use as much as 15 litres per flush.

Where the waste pipe between the U-bend and the pit or tank is more than 2m in length an inspection chamber or **roding point** is needed along its length to allow roding upwards and downwards to prevent blockage (see page 92).

Advantages: Lack of odour; ideal where water is used for anal-cleansing; easy to clean; off-set design does not require a self-supporting latrine slab.

Constraints: Increased quantity of water required; solid anal-cleansing materials may cause blockages; more expensive than simple pit latrines.

See **Appendix 4.6** for a bill of quantities for a pour-flush latrine.

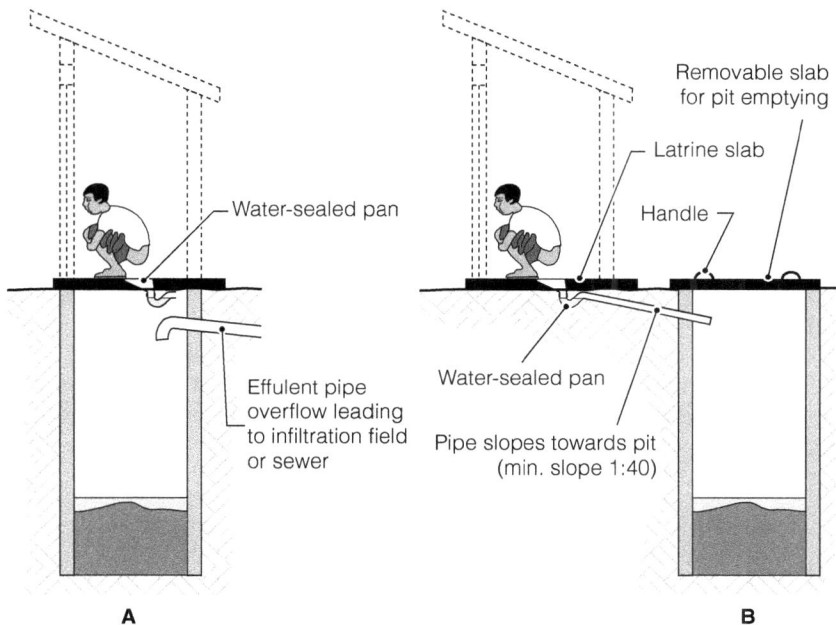

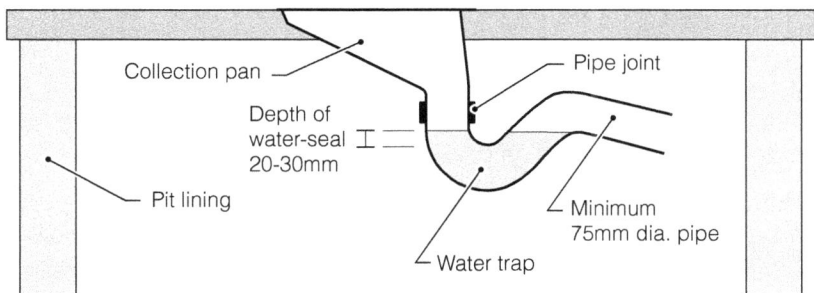

Figure 5.5. Pour-flush latrines

5.6 Septic-tanks

Where several pour-flush latrines are required these may be used in conjunction with a septic-tank. A septic-tank is designed to collect and treat toilet wastewater and other grey water. Its use is likely to be appropriate where the volume of wastewater produced is too large for disposal in pit latrines, and water-borne sewerage is uneconomic or unaffordable. Septic-tanks are, therefore, particularly suited to systems involving high water use, especially where water is used for flushing and anal-cleansing. However, they are difficult to manage for large populations and are best suited to single households or institutions such as hospitals or schools.

Wastes from toilets, and sometimes kitchens and bathrooms, pass though pipes to a watertight tank where they are partially treated. After one to three days the liquid wastes leave the tank and are carried to a secondary treatment system. This is usually some form of underground disposal system (such as an infiltration field), sewer or secondary-treatment facility.

The treatment process in a septic-tank occurs in four stages:

Settlement: Heavy solids settle to the base of the tank to form a sludge which must occasionally be removed; about 80 per cent of the suspended solids can be separated from the liquid in a well-designed tank.

Flotation: Grease and oil float to the surface to form a layer of scum; over time this scum layer becomes thick and the surface may be hard.

Sludge digestion and consolidation: The sludge at the bottom of the tank is compressed by the weight of new material settling on top, increasing its density; and organic matter in the sludge and scum layers is broken down by bacteria which convert it to liquid and gas.

Stabilization: The liquid in the tank undergoes some natural purification but the process is not complete; the final effluent is anaerobic and will contain pathogenic organisms such as roundworm and hookworm eggs.

The final effluent leaving the septic-tank will still be full of pathogens and must be disposed of in an appropriate location such as a soakaway pit, infiltration field or sewerage system. All septic-tanks require a system for removing the sludge and disposing of it hygenically (see Section 8.7).

Detailed design details for septic-tanks can be found in Section 7.7.

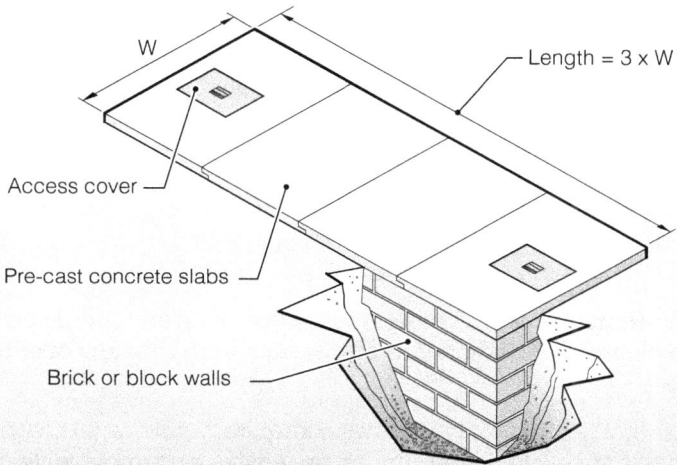

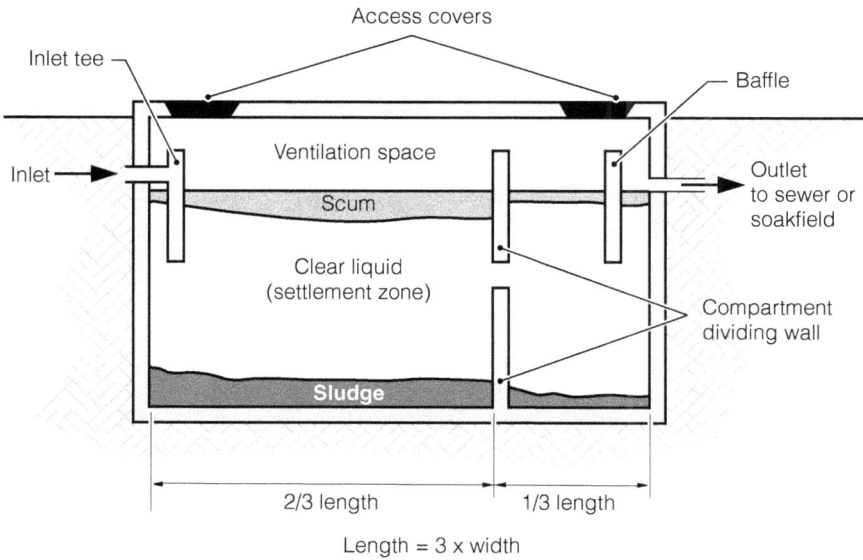

Figure 5.6. Septic-tank

5.7 Communal aqua-privies

An aqua-privy is simply a latrine constructed directly above a septic-tank. Aqua-privies are appropriate where pit latrines are socially or technically unacceptable but the volume of sullage is small. The amount of water required for flushing is much smaller than for a septic-tank due to the location of the tank. The water-seal pan and extension of the drop pipe 75mm below the water surface helps to exclude odours from the super-structure. The tank of the aqua privy must be watertight to maintain a constant liquid level in the tank. The outlet pipe should extend at least 50mm below the water surface to provide an odour seal.

Advantages: Reduced odour; ideal where water is used for anal-cleansing; easy to clean; more efficient to empty tank than for individual pour-flush latrines.

Constraints: Increased quantity of water required; solid anal-cleansing materials may cause blockages; more expensive and more difficult to construct than simple pit latrines.

An alternative to the communal aqua-privy is the open drain communal latrine (pictured) whereby pour-flush pans discharge directly into a sewage pipe which feeds a septic-tank.

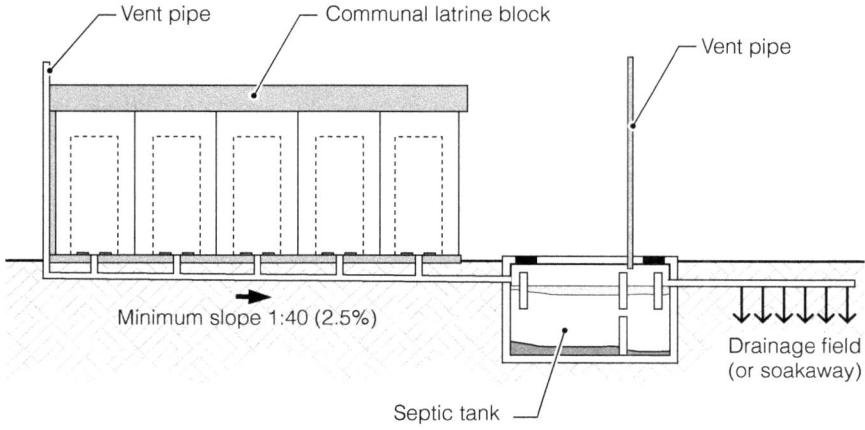

Open drain communal latrine

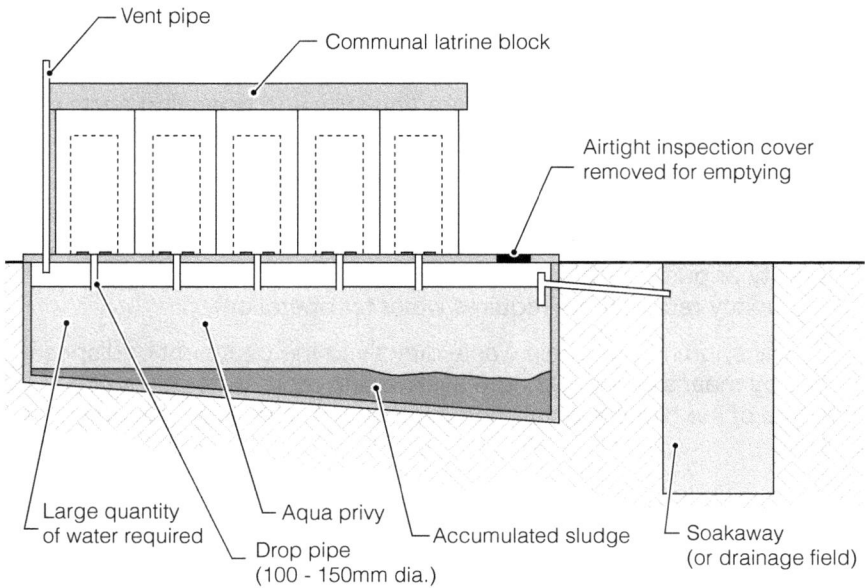

Figure 5.7. Communal aqua-privy

85

5.8 Wastewater treatment systems

In most emergency situations it is possible to use on-site excreta disposal systems whereby human wastes are disposed of without treatment. In some cases, however, it is necessary to treat wastewater prior to disposal. This occurs most often in densely populated areas where traditional on-site solutions cannot be implemented. These include urban environments, rocky terrains that do not allow pits to be dug, where prevention of groundwater contamination is crucial, or where there is simply a cultural resistance to low-technology solutions.

The most simple wastewater treatment system is the septic-tank (as described in Section 5.6) but there are also more advanced treatment technologies that can be used to treat larger volumes of sewage.

Collection and transport

Wastewater treatment systems achieve safe excreta disposal by first collecting and transporting the waste from the toilets. This requires a much smaller area that that required for in-situ solutions providing on-site disposal of excreta such as pit latrines. Collection and transport can be done essentially in one of three ways:

- by temporarily storing the excreta in appropriate tanks and frequently emptying these by vacuum trucks (logistics and operating costs may be a problem with this as is the case with chemical toilets);

- by settling part of the waste in an arrangement similar to a septic-tank and transporting the liquid portion of the waste to the treatment or disposal site by means of a small bore sewerage system by gravity or pumping (this considerably reduces the emptying frequency required but requires water for operation); or

- by transporting the whole waste directly to the treatment or disposal site by means of a larger bore system and more water (these have some of the highest installation costs and require large amounts of water).

Treatment and disposal

The waste, once collected and transported to a more suitable site, may be either disposed of as it is, or treated before disposal into a watercourse or pit. Simple disposal is not recommended due to the high pathogen content of the waste and some form of wastewater treatment is usually required with emphasis on pathogen reduction. Having said this, direct disposal may be the only option in the initial stages of an emergency, and the risk may be mitigated by the addition of lime to pits.

All wastewater treatment systems produce sludge as part of the treatment process either continuously or intermittently. This sludge requires careful handling and can be disposed of in a pit, an incinerator or on agricultural land. See Section 8.7 for more details on sludge disposal.

Commercial systems

There are several package wastewater treatment units available on the market. The main types are:

Rotating Biological Contactors (RBCs) which treat the waste by having many disks mounted on a shaft which rotates slowly to alternatively submerge and aerate the biomass on these disks.

Biological Aerated Filters or Submerged Aerated Filters (BAF/SAFs) which rely on mobile or fixed submerged media in a tank where the biomass is attached and is continuously aerated from diffusers underneath it.

Membrane Bioreactors (MBRs) which rely on submerged membranes within an aerated tank that essentially filter the incoming wastewater.

Activated Sludge processes which again rely on continuous aeration followed by a settling stage to recover the biomass. All-in-one tank batch versions of this process exist and are called Sequencing Batch Reactors (SBRs).

Advantages:

- highly automated units which require little maintenance and attention;
- quick to install as they usually come in containerized or trailer-mounted units;
- generally, good performance with built-in disinfection; and
- membranes provide a physical barrier against pathogens.

Constraints:

- very expensive for the population served, typically over $85 per person served;
- generally only suitable for small populations;
- high energy requirements as most are based on aerated processes for compactness;
- require experienced personnel for installation and skilled workers to deal with the electronic controls;
- not designed to treat the highly concentrated waste arising from emergency settlements as this may inhibit their performance; and
- SAFs, BAFs and, to a certain extent, RBCs are not suitable for operation with intermittent power supplies.

5.9 Excreta disposal for institutions

In many emergency situations there is a need to provide excreta disposal facilities for institutions such as hospitals, feeding centres and schools. These will be communal facilities but are normally constructed to a higher standard than domestic communal facilities. In determining the design and layout of instutional facilities, the following factors should be considered:

Segregation: Toilet facilities for males and females must be segregated and situated in different parts of the institution's grounds to ensure privacy for women and girls. The number of cubicles required for males can be reduced by building urinals. A ratio of 3 to 1 for female to male cubicles is a useful guideline.

Convenience: Facilities should be near enough to the buildings of the institution to ensure that they are used. A **maximum distance of 50m** is recommended.

Accessibility: Toilets must be easily accessible to the very young, very old, the weak and infirm, and disabled people. This is especially important for hospitals and schools.

Handwashing facilities: Handwashing facilities should be provided alongside latrines. Ideally, there should be **1 tap for every 4 cubicles**.

Privacy: Handwashing facilities for women and girls should be surrounded by a privacy wall or situated inside to enable them to wash sanitary cloths.

Security: Where possible, facilities should not be right next to a fence or institutional boundary where the user may be afraid of intimidation or abuse.

Operation and maintenance: Staff should be employed by the institution to ensure that facilities are used and maintained in an appropriate fashion.

Design: When sizing pits, sludge accumulation rates should be adjusted based on the number of days and hours spent at the institution. The following equation can be used:

Where: d = number of days per week at institution

w = number of weeks per year at institution

$$\text{Adjusted sludge accumulation rate (AS)} = \frac{(d \times w \times h) \times S}{24 \times 365}$$

h = number of hours per day at institution

S = standard sludge accumulation rate (l/person/year)

This can have a big impact on the design of facilities. For example, where a school is attended for 6 hours a day and 5 days a week for 42 weeks of the year, a 'standard' sludge rate of 40 litres/person/day may be reduced 6 litres/person/day by applying this equation.

See Section 7.3 for more details of sludge accumulation rates and pit-sizing details.

There is a range of latrine types that can be used for institutions, including trench latrines, VIP latrines, communal pour-flush latrines (discharging to a septic-tank as in Figure 5.8) and aqua-privies. In general, toilet blocks consisting of four to six cubicles are easiest to construct and maintain.

School latrines

School latrines can be made 'child-friendly' by incorporating certain design features, including:

- squat toilets with smaller, 'child-size' holes;

- for younger children, toilets can be open (i.e. with no walls separating them), meaning friends can talk while using the toilet instead of being in a small, dark enclosure;

- providing for child-friendly colourful artwork on the sides of the superstructures; and

- ensuring cubicle interiors are well-lit.

Table 5.1 summarizes the recommended **minimum** number of users per toilet for schools (in all cases numbers should be rounded up).

Schools can also be used to impart hygiene promotion messages to pupils and determine baseline behaviours. Children can be effective facilitators for hygiene promotion – passing on messages to other children and family members.

Intervention agencies can work with schools and local communities to instigate sustainable school sanitation programmes (see Box 5.2).

Table 5.1. Minimum toilet provision for schools

Group	Females	Males
Nursery-school children Age: 3 - 5 yrs	1 cubicle per 20 users + 1	1 cubicle per 20 users + 1
Primary-school children Age: 5 - 12 yrs	1 cubicle per 30 users + 1	1 cubicle per 40 users 1 urinal space per 40 users
High-school children Age: 12 - 18 yrs	1 cubicle per 30 users + 1	1 cubicle per 50 users 1 urinal space per 40 users
Teaching staff	1 cubicle per 10 users (with a minimum of 2)	1 cubicle per 10 users

Source: Deverill and Still, 1998

Box 5.2.

Providing school latrines in East Timor

As a first step in developing a latrine design for schools in East Timor, an NGO instigated a consultative process with the Ministry of Education (MoE), the Ministry of Health (MoH), Water Supply and Sanitation (WSS), community leaders such as the aldeia chiefs and headmasters, as well as potential users of the water systems, in order to assess the water and sanitation needs of target schools. Discussions included the project objectives, the respective responsibilities of all stakeholders, the history of each school (including the destruction in 1999), and the community's views on any operational challenges that may be faced during implementation. An operational plan was developed based on these discussions.

Where a school was close to a community, discussions were held with each community and the relevant headmasters regarding the formation of a Water Management Committee (WMC). These meetings focused on the responsibilities expected of the WMCs/ headmasters and the difference between the present political and social situation compared to the Indonesian-controlled times. The NGO pledged technical training and organizational support to the WMCs while the community acknowledged their responsibility for the health of their children through the maintenance of the water-supply and sanitation facilities. A commitment to establish WMCs was obtained from these discussions.

Prior to the construction of facilities, meetings were held between the NGO and community representatives to discuss the most suitable facilities to be installed, as well as the most suitable WMC organizational structure to be established. The responsibilities of each member of the WMC were decided jointly and the WMC formally established with open and transparent proceedings. Community-recognized WMCs were formed to manage and maintain facilities in all communities linked to schools.

Source: ECHO Final Narrative Report – Water, Sanitation and Hygiene for East Timorese Children, 2001 – 2002

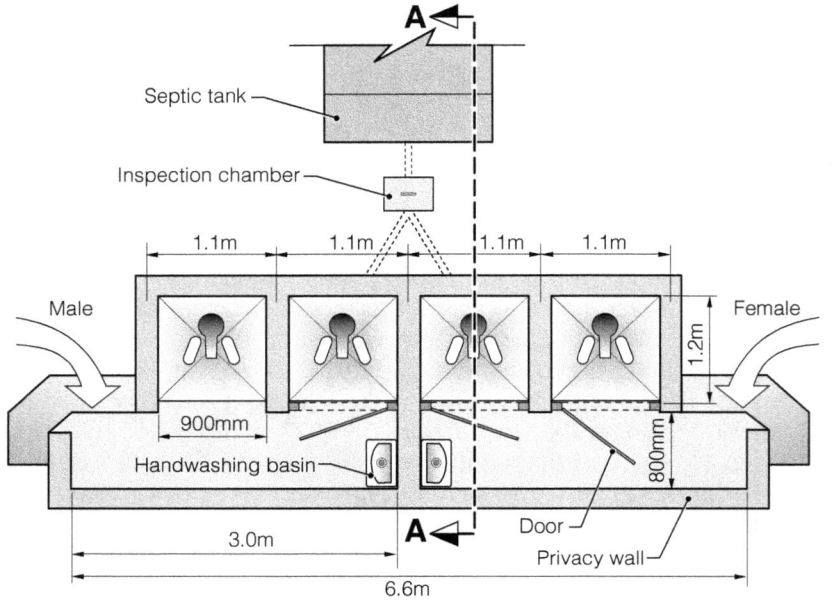

Plan view

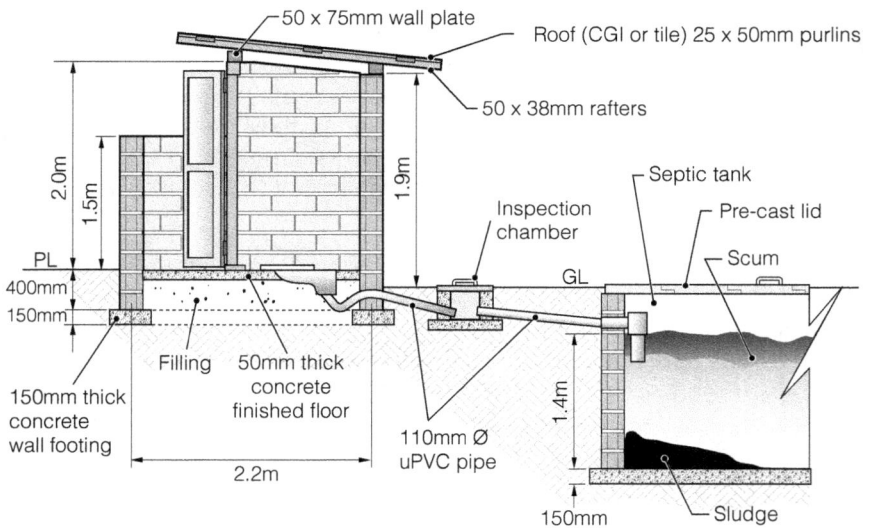

Section on A-A

Figure 5.8. Institutional latrine design

6.

Strategies for Difficult Situations

This chapter presents a range of technical options for 1st and 2nd phase emergency implementation for difficult situations. It should be used to identify possible solutions for a specific situation. The final choice of option should be decided upon only after CONSULTATION with the intended users.

In some situations there may be specific challenges which make implementation of an emergency excreta disposal programme especially difficult, making it impossible to use traditional technologies.

Such difficult situations include:

- where the water-table is very close to the ground surface, limiting excavation;

- where groundwater sources are likely to be contaminated easily;

- where there is hard rock close to the surface, making excavation very difficult;

- where people are used to water-based systems but the soil and ground is non-absorbent;

- where the ground is so soft that pit walls collapse before an adequate depth can be reached;

- in crowded peri-urban or urban environments where there is little available space and limited accessibility;

- in flood-affected areas; and

- where toilets are not wanted or accepted by the community.

The technical solutions for excreta disposal in difficult situations, such as those described above, are limited. If conditions are obviously unsuitable a strong case may need to be made to support the movement of people to a more suitable site. However, often there is no other option to these sites and alternative solutions will need to be found.

6.1 High water-tables

Generally, the base of the pit must be at least 1.5m above the wet-season water-table to prevent contamination, but in some geological conditions this may be insufficient. If there is a conflict between latrine provision and water supply it is usually easier and cheaper to develop another water source than to provide alternative excreta disposal facilities. This may not always be possible, however, and wherever the groundwater level is high, protective measures should be taken, especially where groundwater is used as a source of drinking water.

In situations where the groundwater is less than 1m from the surface it is virtually impossible to prevent contamination of the groundwater, therefore greater attention should be paid to ensuring that people do not drink water from shallow wells without treating the water in some way.

If groundwater resources are not exploited for water supply in the area, the prevention of groundwater contamination should be of secondary importance to the provision of adequate excreta disposal facilities.

Where the water-table is high **and** groundwater is used as a water source, there are a number of excreta disposal options that can be applied, including:

* **Raised pit latrines** – widespread solution, relatively simple to construct, require emptying, may be single or twin-pit;

* **Sand-enveloped pit latrines** – relatively time-consuming to construct, require suitable sand, can be combined with a raised pit;

* **Sealed pits or tanks** – must be water-tight, can be above or below ground, relatively expensive;

* **Dehydrating or composting latrines** – can be raised or shallow twin-pit, work best where people are already accustomed to their use or where there is agricultural activity; and

- **Septic-tanks or aqua-privies** – can be above or below ground, relatively expensive, require water and space.

Raised pit latrines

The most common solution for excreta disposal in areas of high water-table is to build raised pit latrines. These can be in the form of simple pit latrines or VIP latrines in which the pit is built upwards above ground level using bricks, blocks, stone, concrete rings, corrugated-iron culverts or earth-covered bamboo or wood reinforced mounds (see Figures 6.1 and 6.2 for examples). This increases cost and construction time considerably and family members may be unable to construct this type of latrine by themselves. To prevent contamination of groundwater, the bottom of the pit should be **at least** 1.5m above the water-table level. It is especially important to know how many people will be using the latrines and to calculate the rate of solid and liquid accumulation in the pit, to size them appropriately. A large number of small-capacity latrines, wide rather than deep, are preferable to fewer large-capacity latrines.

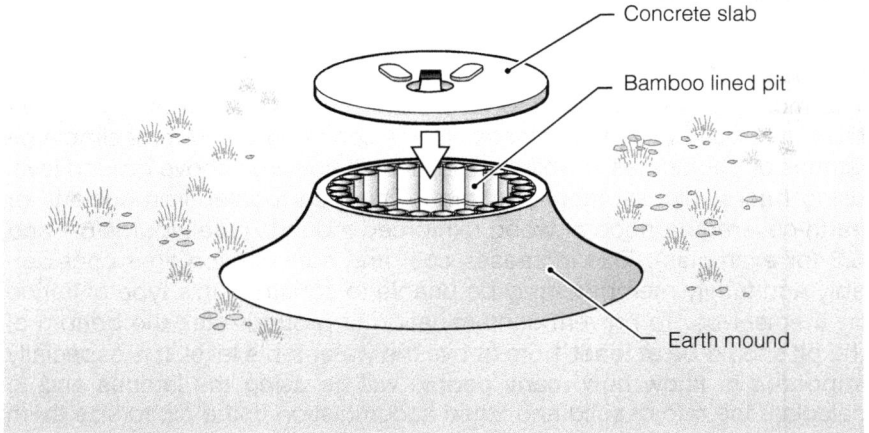

Concrete slab

Bamboo lined pit

Earth mound

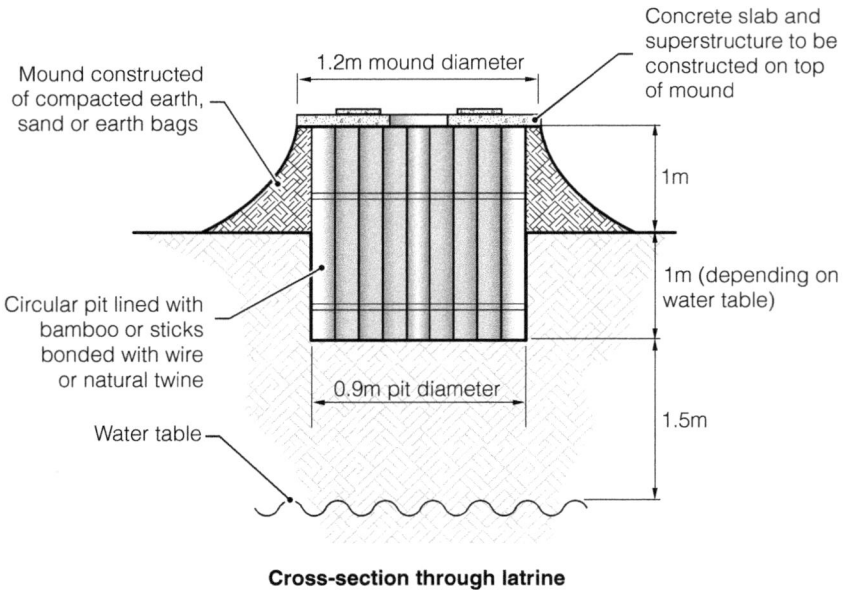

Mound constructed of compacted earth, sand or earth bags

1.2m mound diameter

Concrete slab and superstructure to be constructed on top of mound

1m

1m (depending on water table)

Circular pit lined with bamboo or sticks bonded with wire or natural twine

0.9m pit diameter

Water table

1.5m

Cross-section through latrine

Figure 6.1. Raised bamboo lined latrine

Plan view

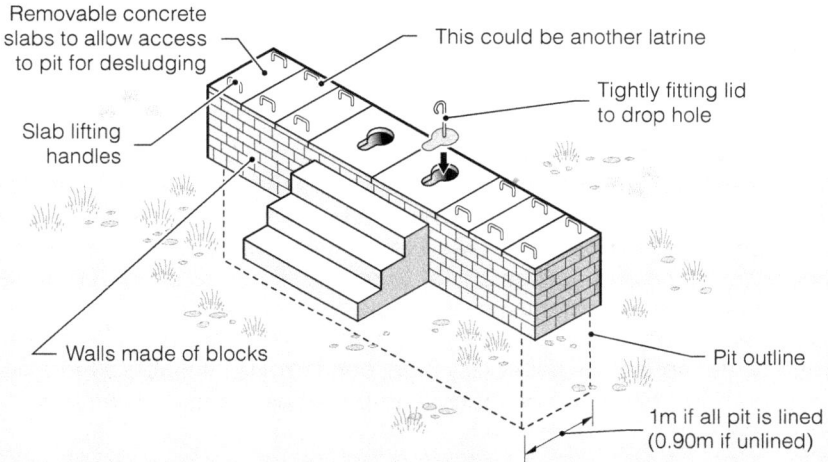

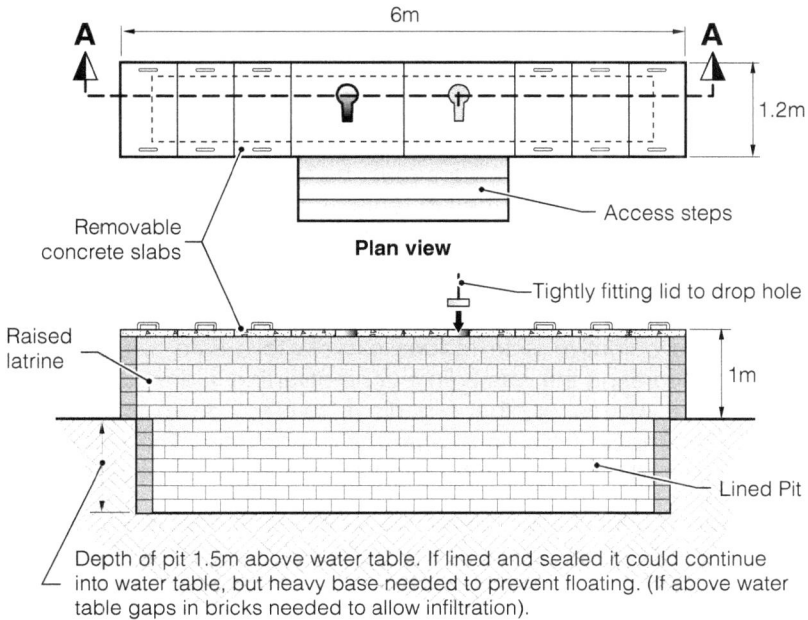

Cross section on A-A

Figure 6.2. Raised block latrine

Using the same concept as the raised pit latrine, mounds or platforms could be built whereby people can defecate directly into buckets or drums which can be emptied manually.

Sand-enveloped pit latrines

Where there is a high risk of groundwater contamination, and it is important to prevent this, a sand envelope can be constructed around a lined latrine pit to reduce pollution (see Figure 6.3). This envelope is usually about 0.5m thick and acts as a filter to minimize the transmission of disease-causing micro-organisms. It should not be assumed that this will stop contamination completely. Where the risk of pollution of nearby groundwater sources is especially high, and there is no viable alternative, it may be appropriate to construct sand-enveloped raised pit latrines.

Eco-San and twin-pit latrines

Eco-San latrines can be used in areas of shallow groundwater. These normally consist of two chambers and are raised above the ground to facilitate easy emptying. One chamber is used until it is full, at which point it is sealed and the second chamber is used. If the contents of the first are left to stand for 1-2 years the waste will be relatively safe to handle and the pit can be emptied. Chambers must be sized so that each takes 1-2 years to fill in order to allow the contents of the first to decompose while the second is being used. Once both pits are full the first can then be emptied and used again.

Eco-San latrines can be urine-diverting or non-urine-diverting (see Section 5.3). The objective is to reduce excreta to a safe re-usable state, either by dehydrating the waste (in a urine-diverting latrine) or by encouraging bacteria, worms, or other organisms to break down organic matter to produce compost (in a non-urine-diverting latrine). The final product can then be used for soil conditioning for agricultural purposes.

Eco-San is most successful in emergency situations where the users are already accustomed to its use and there is significant agricultural activity in the area. Even where this is not the case, however, it can sometimes be used in areas of shallow groundwater if an appropriate consultation process is followed (see Box 6.1).

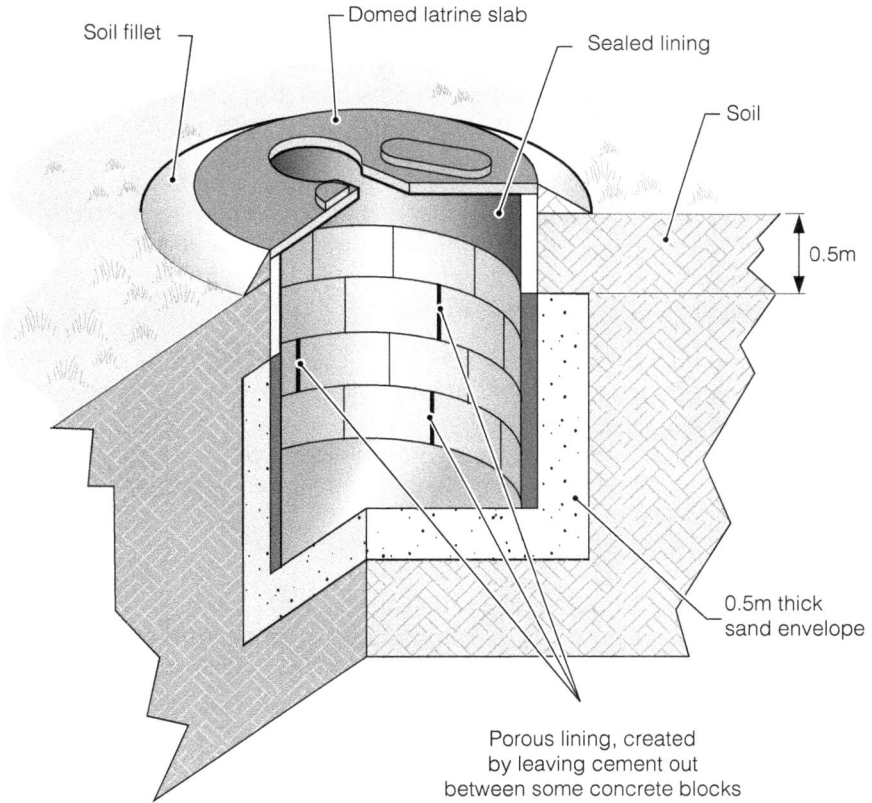

Figure 6.3. Sand-enveloped latrine

Box 6.1.

Twin-pit composting latrines in Nepal

In March 1992 around 90,000 people fled persecution in Bhutan and became refugees in the lowlands of Eastern Nepal. An initial rapid assessment indicated that communal latrines were not proving to be very effective with widespread evidence of open defecation and pollution of shallow tube wells. Following consultation, it was decided that twin-pit composting latrines should be constructed in order to deal with the shallow water-table, each shared between two families so that they would take responsibility and feel ownership of latrines and so that solids accumulation did not exceed shallow-pit capacity.

The immediate impacts of this decision included:

- moving from communal latrines to shared family latrines initially reduced and, subsequently, virtually eliminated open defecation;
- in conjunction with improvements in water supply and hygiene promotion, health problems related to excreta-related diseases started to decrease to manageable levels.

Longer-term impacts included:

- health improved to an acceptable level for the area;
- over a nine-year period, latrine costs were kept to an affordable level as investments are only required for maintenance;
- local government and other agencies were very satisfied with the latrine design – which was subsequently introduced to local communities in villages surrounding the camps;
- the refugee community was very satisfied with the latrine design and most participated in pit emptying on a voluntary basis.

Composting latrines were introduced to communities with no previous knowledge of such systems, initially for technical reasons, but with results that were not expected by many people. These latrines have proved to be popular with the users over many years without major change or problems occurring. In this regard the decision to choose this design early on was the right one.

Double-vault Eco-San latrines should be designed so that the time taken to fill one vault or pit is one to two years. Where it is not feasible to dig a deep pit, it may be easier and cheaper to dig several shallow pits side by side and move the latrine superstructure. If groundwater almost reaches the ground surface, or there is a risk of flooding, both excreta chambers can be constructed entirely above ground (see Box 6.2). Twin-pits can also be used in conjunction with VIP latrines or pour-flush latrines where pits can be off-set but still require emptying.

Sealed pits/tanks

Groundwater contamination can also be prevented if the disposal pit or tank is fully lined and sealed, so that the contents are unable to infiltrate into the surrounding ground. This can be done using locally available materials such as concrete, cement blocks, bricks, plastic tanks, Oxfam tanks, and concrete or metal culvert rings. The construction of fully lined pits is expensive and time-consuming, however, and is likely to be impractical where family latrines are desired. The second disadvantage is that such pits will need to be emptied relatively regularly, as no infiltration can occur.

Septic-tanks and aqua-privies

Septic-tanks and aqua-privies can also be used where the water-table is high. These minimize groundwater contamination by reducing pathogens in the waste, especially if the final effluent is discharged on the ground surface of agricultural land. Such systems are most appropriate where water is available in reasonably large quantities and where water is used for anal-cleansing.

Septic-tanks can be constructed above or below ground but, if below ground, the weight of the tank must be sufficient to prevent flotation due to high groundwater. Sufficient weight is most easily achieved by constructing a thick concrete base to the tank. A simple relationship to calculate the depth of concrete required for the base is:

$$\textbf{Depth of concrete base (D)} = \frac{\textbf{Height of tank (H)}}{\textbf{2.4}}$$

(Where the density of concrete is taken as 2.4kg/m^3.)

101

Using this method, a tank of height 1.5m would require a base depth of 0.6m. This method assumes that the ground is completely saturated and that the total hydrostatic uplift will be countered by the weight of the concrete base alone (the walls and roof are not included). Consequently, this method carries a significant degree of safety and may involve significantly more mass concrete than the minimum required.

For a reinforced-concrete septic-tank, a more accurate calculation for a more efficient design is as follows:

$$D = \frac{(LWH/2.4) - 2WHt - 2HLt - LWt - 0.8Ht(W - 2t)}{LW}$$

Where:
- D = minimum depth of concrete base required
- L = total external length of tank
- W = external width of tank
- H = height of tank (without base or roof)
- t = thickness of tank walls

This assumes that all the tank walls (including the dividing chamber wall) and the roof are constructed from reinforced concrete (of density 2.4kg/m^3) and that all the walls are of equal thickness.

An alternative approach to prevent flotation as a result of uplift is to create a width toe by extending the base of the tank on all sides so that it is wider than the walls. For example, for a tank of width 1.0m and length 3.0m, the dimensions of the base might be 1.6m by 3.6m, creating a 300mm lip around the tank walls. The 300mm space around the tank is then filled with soil so that the weight of soil above the edges of the base assists in overcoming uplift. However, this design is more difficult to construct.

Box 6.2.

Elevated compost latrine construction in El Salvador

The first foundation of the latrine – a pit is excavated and filled with rock. Reinforcement iron rods are placed around the pit and a second 3/8" reinforcement is placed where the prepared concrete blocks (100 x 200 x 400mm) are arranged.

Structure of the latrine is raised with concrete blocks and steps going up to a reinforced-concrete floor.

Completed latrine with two polyethlyene seats and a zinc-aluminum laminate superstructure.

6.2 Flooding

Flood disasters as a result of hurricanes, cyclones and heavy rainfall may lead to enormous human suffering, loss of life and economic damage. There are different types of flooding events that cause different problems; we can define three main types of flood:

- **Rapid-onset floods** – these include flash floods, tidal surges, high runoff from heavy rainfall, dam bursts and overtopping, canals and rivers bursting their banks; typically water rises to dangerous levels within 48 hours.

- **Slow-onset floods** – prolonged rainfall causing low-lying areas to gradually become flooded over a matter of days or weeks.

- **Annual seasonal flooding** – many communities around the world are flooded annually and may be under water for some considerable time each year.

While the majority of deaths associated with flooding are directly attributable to rapid-onset floods, many deaths also occur from diseases immediately after flood events as a result of unsanitary environments and contaminated water. Good and appropriate excreta disposal in these situations can have a profound effect on the health of the affected populations.

To ensure an environment free from faecal contamination, three main areas must be addressed:

1. promotion of good excreta disposal practices by the affected population through the involvement of the community in the design and siting of the latrines;

2. prevention of overflowing of raw sewage from pits and septic tanks during flooding which would result in a very serious environmental-health hazard; and

3. provision of adequate excreta disposal facilities for displaced people during flooding.

Particularly if sanitation systems are already inadequate, flooding can have **serious consequences**. Sewage may be washed into houses and damage to sanitation systems can contaminate water supplies. The combined effects of open sewage and reduced opportunities for good personal hygiene also favour the spread of infections causing diarrhoea, such as cholera and gastrointestinal viruses. Countries with a good infra-structure for drainage and disposal of human waste have far fewer direct health problems during flood disasters, showing the importance of taking measures for disaster preparedness.

Flood-response strategy

There is no single solution for excreta disposal in response to a rapid-onset flood event. The optimum solution will depend on local cultural practices, environmental issues and what local materials are available for use.

Public consultations and awareness programmes are essential to inform people of the possible knock-on effects of floods and establish what it is and isn't possible for the community to do. If a community truly under-stands the enormous public health risks associated with poor sanitation they themselves can often find more creative, low-cost solutions than most NGOs can.

Even in a 1st phase emergency, hygiene and public health promotion is a crucial component of response. The population needs to be involved in decision-making and implementation as much as possible right from the start. People need to know why it is important to remove or contain the excreta and the different ways in which this can be done. They should be consulted as far as possible on the siting, design and use of any excreta disposal system proposed.

Possible excreta disposal solutions for flood-prone areas for first- and second-phase emergency response are summarized below.

1st Phase options for rapid-onset floods

- **Over-hung toilets** – in floods where there is still flowing water or a river nearby, one of the quickest ways to eliminate the public health risk is to excrete directly in the river. Before this option is selected it is essential that a sanitary survey of downstream water use is conducted to ensure that it does not present a major health risk for people downstream. Cubicles should be quickly erected for this as in most cultures privacy is a major concern, especially for women. It is also important that construction is sound and that latrines are accessible and safe for users including young children, the elderly and disabled people.

- **Floating latrines** – similar in principle to over-hung latrines, floating latrines are designed so that faeces fall directly into a river or into floodwaters. The base of the latrine superstructure is commonly made from timber/bamboo so that it floats like a raft (see Photograph 6.1).

- **Portable chemical toilets** (Section 4.8) – this is an expensive short-term option and depends on the local availability of such toilets. Chemical toilets require regular servicing and emptying and a contractor to do this; it is also necessary to have a flat, stable surface on which to place each unit.

- **Bucket latrines** (Section 4.6) – a number of large buckets/containers or barrels with squatting slabs of some sort over the top can be set up so people can defecate in them. These need to be provided in makeshift cubicles, using cloth, plastic sheeting or local building materials, and need to be emptied daily. A safe system of bucket collection and final disposal of excreta is essential if this option is to have minimal negative impacts.

- **Plastic bags** (Section 4.7) – in the immediate aftermath of some flood events, such as those in Bangladesh in 1998, people can defecate in plastic bags and then float them away. This is an emergency short-term measure only and if the bags are not collected and disposed of properly, or a river does not take them out to sea, this would constitute a serious health risk.

- **Temporary dismountable latrines** (Box 6.3) – where flooding has damaged existing sanitation facilities, temporary latrines that can be disassembled after use and reused elsewhere can be constructed locally. These are designed to be assembled above a pit latrine with urine separation to a soakaway. They can also be raised if there is a continued threat of flooding or to prevent groundwater contamination in areas with high water-tables.

Photograph 6.1. Floating latrine in Indonesia

Box 6.3.

Dismountable latrines in flooded areas of Eastern Bolivia

The San Julian region in Eastern Bolivia is prone to periodic flooding. Often, traditional pit latrines and water-flush systems are destroyed by floodwaters following such events. Following recent floods in March 2006, a novel, communal latrine unit was used that can be disassembled and moved to a new location if required. The unit was manufactured locally off-site, and planned for installation in locations such as schools and other community buildings.

The design incorporates two-drop-holes and a urinal for males; two-drop-holes for females, handwashing facilities and an external laundry basin. The unit was designed to be placed on a dry pit 4m long, 0.9m wide and 2.5m deep, and is fitted with four urine-separation toilet bowls connected to a soakaway

Key design features:

- Located in communal buildings
- Dry pit (raised in flood zones)
- Urine-separation toilet pedestal
- Dismountable (can be moved)
- High-quality units
- Integrated handwashing and laundry facilities

2nd Phase options

- **Raised latrines** (Section 6.1) – there is a variety of ways to raise latrines (including using earth, mud bricks, cement blocks and concrete structures depending on what is locally available) and it is normally necessary to raise them by only 1–1.5m above ground level. If this option is selected as part of a flood-response strategy, it is important not to forget the house; if the house is submerged then people will flee their houses anyway. There are numerous examples of excreta disposal programmes where implementing agencies have raised latrines above the level of the users' houses.

- **Sealed pits or tanks** – such pits may need dewatering before construction can go ahead; 1m³ pre-cast ferrocement tanks can usually be manufactured fairly easily or plastic tanks can be used with appropriate fittings for desludging. This is the preferred option for institutions such as schools and hospitals; when used for houses one tank can serve a number of houses. (N.B. These are not septic-tanks since they only contain the waste for a limited period and then need to be emptied. They do not treat sewage prior to discharge to a soakfield or sewerage system, as in a septic-tank.)

- **Raised water-tight tanks** – where there is a need to prevent human excreta being washed into surface water and/or a need to prevent groundwater contamination, raised water-tight tanks may be used. These are constructed above ground and excreta is contained in a water-tight plastic or ferrocement tank. Facilities for desludging are required.

- **Eco-San latrines** (Section 5.3) – not recommended for areas that flood frequently (see Box 6.4) but for where floods have subsided (but digging pits is impossible). Where people do not have a history of excreta reuse, it will take a long time to raise awareness of the process initially and, later, for using the waste when the first container is full.

- **Low-cost sewerage system** – if there is sufficient water available, and large-bore drainage pipes, from 200mm to 3m in diameter, then people can defecate directly into special holes in the pipe, and water will be released periodically to wash the sewage into a sump for desludging or for pumping out to sea. Washing areas could also be plumbed into these sewage drains to help the effluent flow.

Box 6.4.

Elevated compost latrines in Dominican Republic

In the second-phase response to flood-affected communities in Dominican Republic, 210 latrines were built, some for individual families and some shared between three to six families. The public-health promotional work before, during and after the construction was extensive and latrines were generally used properly and kept clean.

The latrines had to be elevated, as the water-table was less than 1m below ground-level, and composting latrines were deemed appropriate as there were other latrines of this design in the area and any other solution involving desludgeable tanks would not be sustainable. The normal rate of solids accumulation was approximately 0.06m³/person/year. Therefore, based on three families comprising 15 people, latrines were designed with a combined volume of the two compartments of 1.44m³, allowing for 20% reduction over a 2-year period.

After one year (or when the first compartment was full) the users were expected to move the toilet pedestal from the drop-hole of the first compartment to the drop-hole of the second. Since the area was prone to flooding, the compartments were sealed with breeze blocks to prevent floodwater entering and to ensure that the contents of the compartment were kept dry to facilitate adequate decomposition. Users were expected to crack open the breezeblocks of the first compartment to remove the compost and then reseal them.

There was concern over whether people would cement up the breezeblocks once they had cracked them open to extract the compost. Some felt that some kind of door or panel might have been more appropriate and sustainable than sealing with blocks, while others argued that this would not be watertight. This illustrates the problem of using composting latrines in flood-prone areas.

- **Small-bore sewage systems** – in crowded settlements prone to flooding, small-bore sewage systems can remove the sewage from densely populated areas but, unless this is constructed properly, it can be prone to flooding itself. Many developing countries also face the problem of lack of sewage treatment for these low-cost systems.

- **Sewage-treatment system** (Section 5.8) – on-surface package wastewater treatment systems can also be used in flood-affected areas, but these are relatively high-tech, high-cost solutions.

Where latrines are situated in areas prone to seasonal flooding, the **pits need to be sealed** to stop the sewage mixing with the groundwater and polluting water sources. This can be done with cement-plastered bricks or blocks, ferrocement or concrete rings. Where flooding can be excessive, **tight-fitting lids should be put on the squat-hole** so that the sewage cannot rise up out of the hole. **Water-seals** can also be used to prevent solids escaping when the tank/pit has become waterlogged.

In some cases flood events can actually have a positive effect by encouraging people to use latrines (see Box 6.5).

Box 6.5.

Flooding as an impetus for latrine use in Nepal

A survey of flood-affected areas in Nepal found that less than 50% of the affected population initially had access to toilets. However, changes in their environment as a result of flooding, such as relocation of villages, denial of access to forests and riversides by the Government – and refusal by landowners to allow defecation on their land – resulted in an unprecedented acceptance and demand for latrines at the village level, even among groups who had never previously used latrines.

6.3 Rocky areas

The solutions suggested for high water-table and flood-affected areas are also applicable to rocky areas.

In addition, for first-phase emergency response in areas where the ground is extremely rocky – making it virtually impossible to dig trenches or cover faeces with soil – **intensive defecation areas** may be needed. In this case a defecation area is set up and each time a person goes to use it they are given a shovel with a cupful of burned lime to take with them. They then sprinkle half of the lime on the sand before defecating on top. The rest of the lime is used to cover the faeces, which are then scooped up on the shovel and taken out to be put in a covered container at the side of the fenced-off area. Staff empty the containers into an off-site pit, or load them onto a truck for disposal elsewhere. As with other public toilet facilities, water and soap should be provided at the defecation area for washing hands. When the sand layer becomes depleted as users scoop up faeces, it should be covered again. This method was used in Goma in 1994.

Also in Goma in 1994, people were encouraged to use existing fissures in the rock for excreta disposal. However, these became full very rapidly. If using rock fissures, extra care should be taken that it is not likely to contaminate an aquifer, especially where groundwater is used for drinking. If mechanical diggers are available, larger pits can be excavated in soft and brittle rock and can be adapted into septic-tanks.

6.4 Urban environments

It is particularly difficult to provide effective excreta disposal when working in a large urban environment. Normally, the first strategy is to make use of or rehabilitate any existing latrines; this may involve isolating part of the sewer system if some parts are damaged. If the sewer is still in operation, a simple emergency option is to construct drop-hole latrines directly over open inspection covers, to allow excreta to drop directly into the sewer. If there is insufficient wastewater discharge to flush the sewer, water tankers can be used to flush them once or twice a day.

If there is large-scale damage to the sewerage system, attempts should be made to locate septic-tanks and set up temporary latrines which feed into them. In some situations it may be possible to hire portable toilets, but these require desludging almost daily in crowded sites, and should only be considered if regular desludging can be guaranteed.

Another technical solution is to use concrete culverts, by blocking off the ends of a row of culverts, digging them in to the ground and making squat-holes in the top of the culverts. If set on a slight gradient, the 'tube' can be desludged from one end. Tanks such as Oxfam tanks can also be dug into the ground and used as desludgeable excrement containers.

Emergency wastewater treatment systems can also be used in urban environments (see Section 5.8), though this is rarely the most appropriate option.

In urban areas it is better to concentrate on communal areas such as markets or transit centres rather than attempt to provide family latrines for everyone. Discussions with community groups should help to identify where the risks are and whether there are possible solutions, such as several families sharing one latrine or public latrines at key locations.

Sewerage systems

Sewerage systems are not common in emergency situations, although they may be used where the affected population remains or relocates in an urban area. Most sewerage systems need at least 20 to 40 litres of water per user per day to be flushed into the system (Adams, 1999). In addition, pumped sewerage systems and sewage-treatment works may require a back-up power supply to keep the system running. This may be a major undertaking.

Where it is necessary to construct a small-scale sewerage system, for example, to feed a septic-tank for several households or for an institution, the following design conditions should be noted:

- Sewage pipes below the water-table should be avoided where possible, to prevent ingress of groundwater, or increased groundwater contamination.

- Pipes in unsaturated ground should be laid in a trench with 200mm of sand below and 300mm above.

- Waste pipes should always be situated below water pipes to minimize potential contamination.

- Pipes should have a minimum diameter of 100mm and should be installed with a fall of approximately 1:40. If the use of smaller-diameter pipes is unavoidable, then a greater fall is needed, i.e. about 1:30 for 75mm pipes.

- Roding eyes should be placed at all upstream termini, intersections of pipes, elbows of 45° or greater, high points in the system and every 30m along straight pipe runs. These allow access for the use of rods to prevent and remove blockages.

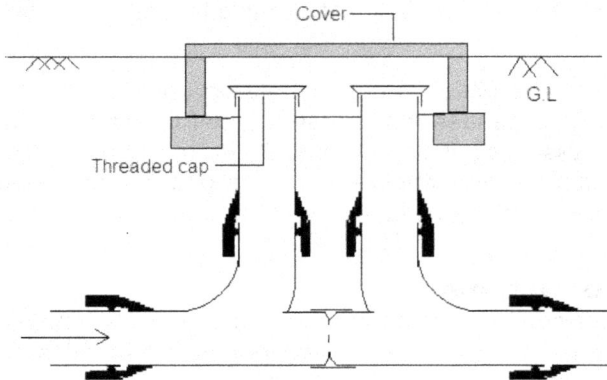

Figure 6.4. Roding eyes - double

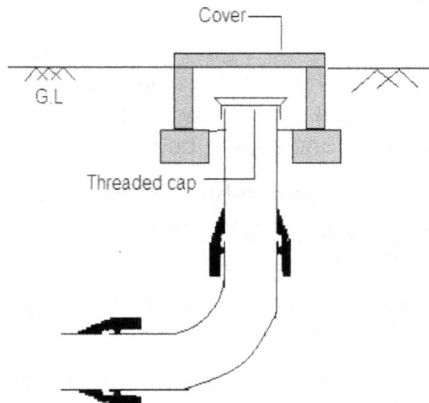

Figure 6.5. Roding eyes - single

- Two or three rocker pipes should be used whenever a pipe exits a static structure to allow for slight movement.

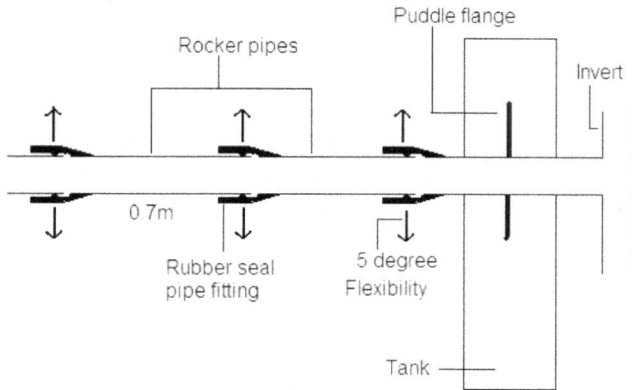

Figure 6.6. Rocker pipes

- If the pipe run has to turn greater than a 90° bend, then turning in 45° stages helps to prevent blockages.

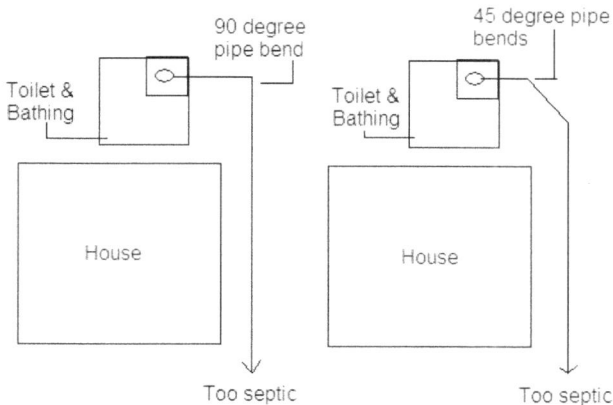

Figure 6.7. 45 Degree pipe bends

See **Appendix 4.10** for a bill of quantities for a sewerage network and infiltration system for five houses.

6.5 Where toilets are not wanted

There can be various situations where people don't want to use toilets or latrines. This normally occurs where latrines are not usually used outside emergency situations and the people themselves do not want to begin using them – or where the local government or landholder does not want to see any form of permanent sanitation system.

The **cat method** is an option for communities who are not familiar with latrines and do not want to use them, such as nomadic communities. This approach encourages people who defecate on the ground to cover up faeces as soon as possible with soil, and provides the necessary tools, such as small hoes, to do this. These hoes provide another incentive to participate in the excreta disposal programme as they can also be used for farming. While other measures are preferable, the cat method is an effective alternative that ensures safe disposal of excreta and does not force latrines on people who do not want them.

Hygiene promotion is particularly important in promoting this method as it emphasizes the importance of covering up faeces so that vectors do not contaminate the local environment. This method can also be used in designated defecation areas along with health promotion and handwashing programmes, or in rural marginalized areas where it is very difficult to obtain any kind of material to construct latrines.

7.

Technical Design Information

This chapter presents supporting technical design information for the options presented in Chapters 4, 5 and 6.

In the design and construction of any latrine it is important to consider the following five key factors:

- Accessibility;
- Safety;
- Comfort and community desires;
- Privacy; and
- Health.

The generic process that should be used in latrine construction is outlined below:

1. Siting of latrine
2. Excavation of pit or disposal system
3. Laying of slab/pedestal and foundations
4. Construction of superstructure
5. Implementation of O&M arrangements
6. Construction of handwashing facilities
7. Determination of monitoring arrangements

7.1 Siting latrines

Perhaps the most important design factor regarding latrine construction is **where** the latrine should be sited. The following factors are important siting selection criteria; each latrine constructed should be:

- not more than 50m away from dwellings to be served;
- at least 30m away from water-storage and treatment facilities;
- at least 30m away from surface water sources;
- at least 30m horizontal distance from shallow groundwater sources (more in coarse or fissured ground – seek local hydrogeological expertise where possible)*;
- downhill of settlements and water sources, where possible;
- at least 50m away from communal food-storage and preparation areas;
- close to handwashing facilities;
- easily accessible to all intended users including children, old people, pregnant women and disabled people.

*While the figure of 30m is often used to indicate the distance that latrines should be from groundwater sources, the required distance can vary greatly depending on ground conditions. A distance equivalent to 25 days travel time is usually sufficient to reduce concentrations of faecal-indicator bacteria (e.g. *E-coli*) to levels where detection within most samples is unlikely (ARGOSS, 2001). Therefore, the 25-day travel distance defines the 'safe' distance from latrines. This distance depends on the soil and rock type. Minimum separation distances for different soil and rock types are given in Table 7.1. As can be seen from the table, 30m separation is adequate for some rock types only; where water flows in fractures within rock, pathogens may be able to travel considerable distances within 25 days and it is not possible to provide a minimum distance in this case.

Siting 'sanitation corridors' parallel to and approximately 10m from dwellings is a useful way to separate accessible sanitation facilities.

Accessibility is a key issue since this is likely to influence how often latrines are used, and hence whether indiscriminate defecation takes place or not. The design and location of toilets must ensure that they are accessible to all relevant vulnerable groups. Security of users, especially women and children, must also be considered, particularly where communal latrines are in place. If necessary, facilities can be lit at night for security and convenience.

Table 7.1. Minimum separation distances for latrines/septic-tanks and groundwater sources

Soil/Rock type	Approximate minimum distance (m)
Silt	10*
Fine silty sand	15
Weathered basement (not fractured)	25
Medium sand	50
Gravel	500
Fractured rocks	Not feasible to use horizontal separation as protection
* 10m is the minimum distance an infiltration system should be from a water source	

7.2 Use of local materials and designs

The single most important factor in the selection of construction materials and tools is local availability. There is often a tendency to focus on the use of typical relief-agency materials, such as plastic sheeting, when there may be much better local alternatives available. It is inefficient and inappropriate to import expensive materials if suitable materials are available locally. Possible construction materials include:

- Wood
- Grass and leaves
- Mud
- Earth blocks
- Bamboo
- Bricks

- Cement
- Gravel
- Sand
- Corrugated-iron (GI) sheets
- Plastic sheeting
- Cloth or sacking

Tools are also often available locally, and although these may sometimes be of lower quality than imported ones, they are likely to be much more cost-effective, and the local population will be more accustomed to using them. Heavy equipment, or specialized equipment, may also be available and this may influence the selected construction method as well as the overall technology choice.

The use of local materials and existing designs is to be encouraged for various reasons. Depending on local resources that are readily available in the local community, they can be deployed immediately for quick construction in the 1st phase of emergency response – typically for traditional pit latrines. As the emergency response progresses and local conditions are monitored, the move towards the use of improved latrines can be considered.

There is also the added benefit that the resulting technology brought in will be viewed by beneficiaries as a local good. This encourages an enhanced sense of community ownership and helps mobilize local communities to undertake repair, maintenance and cleaning.

In many cases community members are capable of designing and constructing their own facilities if they are provided with appropriate tools and technical advice (see Box 7.1). The construction of a demonstration latrine can be a useful way to show people the stages in construction, and for those who have constructed before to share techniques and ideas with other community members. The team supervising and facilitating the process should ensure that basic design principles are followed and that latrines are technically safe.

A system of rotation of toolkits can also be implemented, with each kit being shared between 10-15 households. The kits are signed over to a representative of the local community. The recipient of the toolkit is then responsible for ensuring that all households wishing to construct latrines have access to the tools, and that they are returned when the household has finished, allowing rotation to the next household. Once all the households have finished construction, the majority of the toolkits are then returned to the implementing agency for use in a new community, and approximately 1 kit per 100 latrines constructed is left with the representative of the community. This is to allow newly returning families to be able to construct their own latrines, drawing on the advice and knowledge gained by other community members, and for families to replace their latrines when they are full. A typical community toolkit should consist of:

- 1 shovel
- 1 hoe
- 1 pickaxe
- 1 machete
- 1 metal bucket
- 5m of rope

Experience shows that it can take a family as little as four days to construct a latrine from local materials, two days to dig the pit, and two days to construct the superstructure. A system of support for those who are unable to construct the latrines for themselves – such as the elderly, people with disabilities, or female-headed households – should also be implemented. This aspect of the programme needs to be carefully monitored, to ensure that vulnerable people and their families are not being excluded or exploited.

Box 7.1.

Using local designs for latrine structure in Angola

Following the closure of IDP camps in Angola, people started returning home and a public health programme started within the returned communities. Initially, a methodology similar to that used in the camps was adopted whereby concrete-dome latrine slabs were introduced. The budgetary constraints of the programme allowed only one latrine per 20 people, and with the memory of the problems associated with shared latrines in the camps, communities were unenthusiastic about participating unless a solution could be found to allow each household to construct a latrine of their own.

A community consultation and sensitization process was carried out to gain a better understanding of what was stopping the families from constructing latrines without external support – and to find an alternative solution. This process led to an understanding that the communities were willing and able to construct traditional family latrines using locally available materials, but they required tools and advice in order to do this.

The implementing agency therefore provided toolkits and technical advice and the community began to construct its own latrines. This approach led to high levels of uptake among returning families and allowed know-how and tools to remain in the community, ensuring that newly returning families would have the opportunity to create basic sanitation infrastructure without the need for further external support. The cost of constructing a latrine using local materials was approximately one ninth of the cost of producing the concrete-domed slabs.

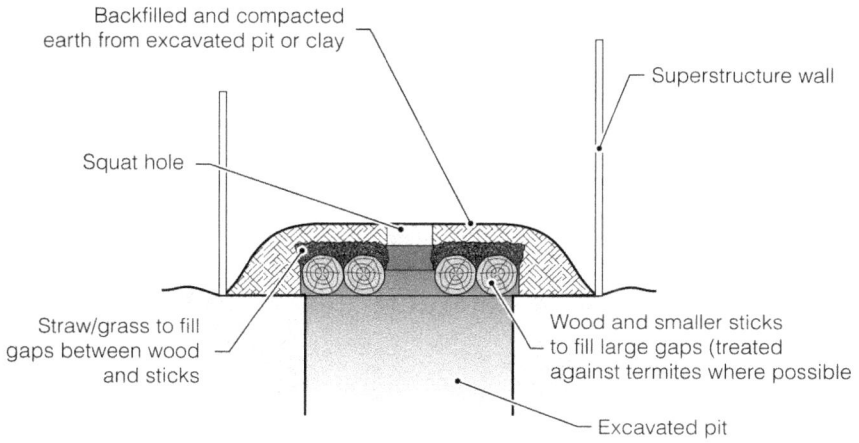

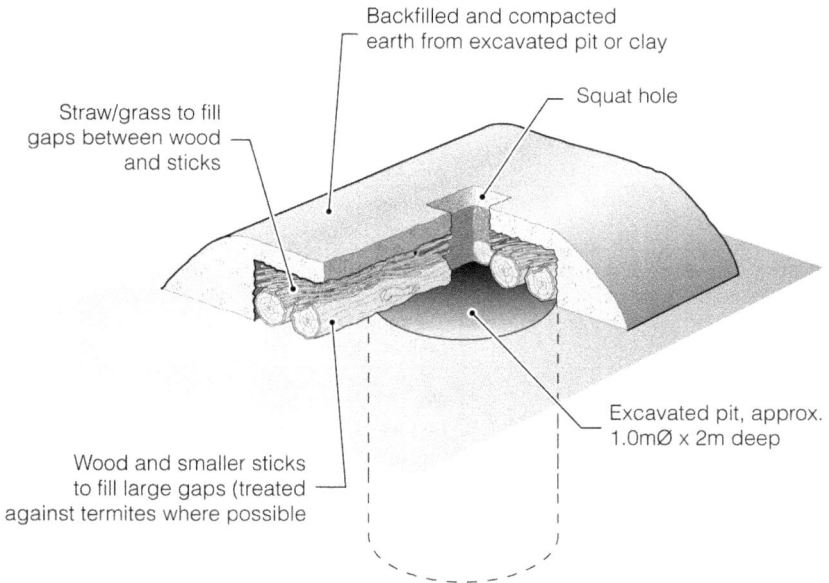

Figure 7.1. Traditional latrine using local materials

Traditional latrine designs typically consist of a pit, a wooden platform packed with grass and covered with soil, and a timber and grass or mud superstructure (see Figure 7.1). A flexible approach should be taken to allow individuals to incorporate their own variations and preferences. Technical guidance should be given regarding:

- the depth of the pit and need for lining;
- the number and size of pieces of wood needed to ensure the stability of the squatting platform; and
- the need to raise the platform above ground level to prevent damage from surface water.

The advantages and disadvantages of a traditional latrine programme using local materials only are summarized in Table 7.2.

Table 7.2. Advantages and disadvantages of traditional latrines

Advantages	Disadvantages/Challenges
Use of locally available materials	Possible contribution to deforestation as trees are harvested to construct the latrine platform; also termites may eat wood unless it is treated with bitumen.
Inexpensive	Cleaning of slab more difficult than with concrete slab.
Replicable: can be constructed by the community themselves, while the knowledge and tools stay within the community.	Reliance on mobilization, and thus reliance on the commitment and acceptance of the implementing agency to promote the methodology.
Flexibility of design and process can be adapted by individuals and communities to suit local preferences.	Not all community members or households will be physically or materially able to construct their own latrine. Solutions to enable such households to participate need to be identified and implemented within target communities.
Adaptation of traditional approach to latrine building means that programme emphasizes the use of local knowledge and skills.	

7.3   Pit excavation and lining

Most single pits for household or family use are about 1m across and 3m deep. It is difficult to excavate pits less than 0.9m diameter because there is not enough room for the person to work. However, there is no maximum size for a pit and sizes vary greatly.

The best shape for a pit (in plan view) is circular. Circular pits are more stable because of the natural arching effect of the ground around the hole – there are no sharp corners to concentrate the stresses. Pits with flat sides are much more likely to need supporting and require a bigger area of lining than a circular pit of the same internal volume. However, many communities prefer to excavate square or rectangular pits as their construction is similar to the process used for building domestic houses.

In general, the **top 0.5m of a pit should always be lined**, but the decision as to whether to line the rest of the pit will depend on the type of soil in which the pit is dug. When a pit is first excavated it may appear stable, and it may be impossible to tell whether or not the walls will collapse after some time. One way in which this can be assessed is to examine other excavations (such as hand-dug wells) in the area. If existing excavations have not collapsed and are not lined, then it is fairly safe to assume that pit-latrine excavations will not need lining. Where there is doubt it is advisable to line the pit. Table 7.3 suggests the types of soil that, in general, do and do not require lining.

Table 7.3. Lining requirements for different soil types

Soils that require lining	Soils that do not require lining
Soft sands and gravels	Soils with significant clay content
Unconsolidated soils	Most consolidated sedimentary rocks
Filled land	Soils with high proportion of iron oxides (laterites)
Compressed mudstones and shales	

The following are commonly used pit-lining materials:

- **Wood** – time-consuming and difficult to position cross-struts to provide a proper retaining wall; prone to rotting even when treated (see Figure 7.2).

- **Concrete blocks** – can be built honeycomb style to allow good infiltration (see Appendix 4.3); circular block moulds can be used for circular pits.

- **Bricks/stone** – time-consuming but may be a preferred alternative to concrete blocks if locally available (see Figure 7.3).

- **Mud blocks** – local alternative to concrete blocks or bricks.

- **Pre-cast concrete rings** – the liquid cannot escape easily unless the ring is made with drainage holes; ring moulds required; expensive (see Figure 7.4).

- **In-situ cast concrete** – relatively time-consuming to construct mould; no infiltration, therefore pits must be emptied; expensive.

- **Sandbags** – sand and bags usually locally available and low cost; cement can be used in bags for stability in areas of shallow groundwater (see Box 7.2).

- **Oil drums** – holes must be made in sides for liquid to infiltrate; small diameter limits diameter of pit size and ease of excavation; corode easily.

- **Ferrocement** – time-consuming and relatively expensive.

- **Corrugated-iron sheets** – very little infiltration can take place unless holes made; need support bracing.

- **Tyres** – requires high quantity of tyres; allows infiltration through spaces and provides stability.

- **Bamboo/cane** – rots faster than wood and less strong – but may be in more plentiful supply in some areas and encourages community participation and income generation (see Box 7.3).

Pit-lining is most cost-effective where pits are to be emptied regularly.

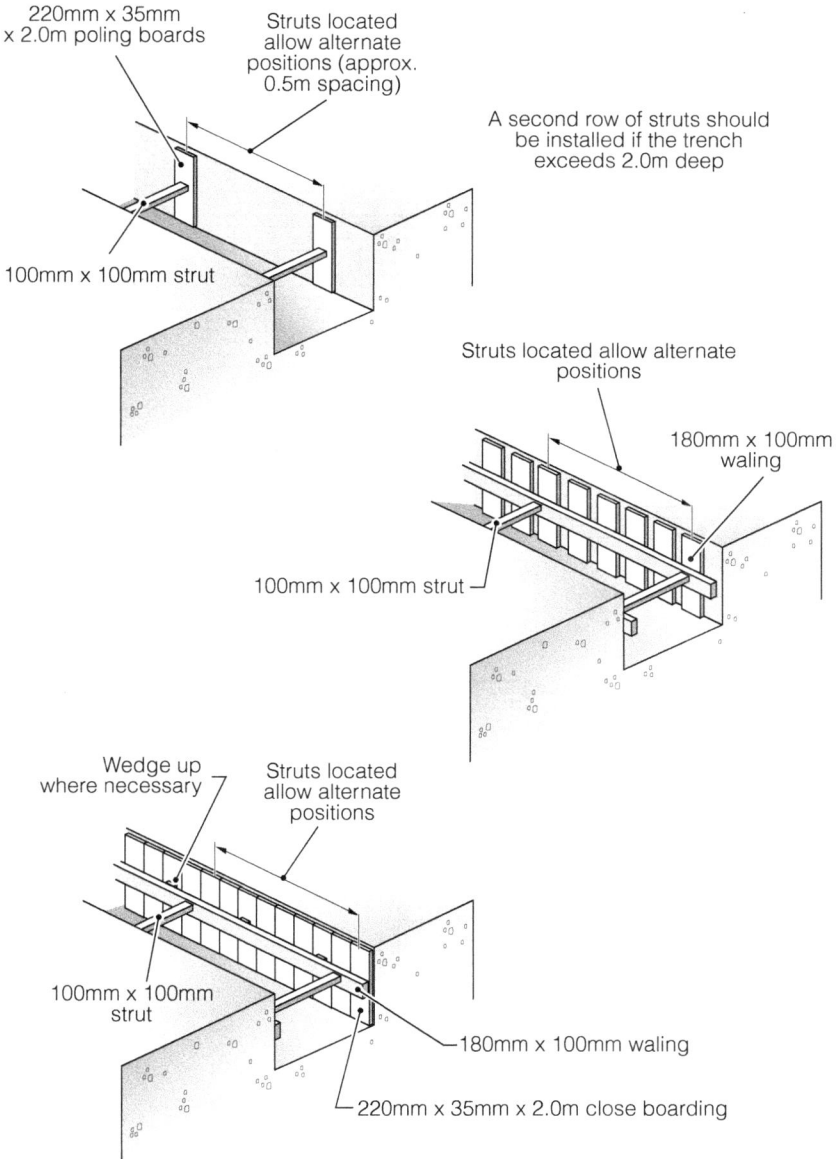

220mm x 35mm x 2.0m poling boards

Struts located allow alternate positions (approx. 0.5m spacing)

A second row of struts should be installed if the trench exceeds 2.0m deep

100mm x 100mm strut

Struts located allow alternate positions

180mm x 100mm waling

100mm x 100mm strut

Wedge up where necessary

Struts located allow alternate positions

100mm x 100mm strut

180mm x 100mm waling

220mm x 35mm x 2.0m close boarding

Figure 7.2. Timber support systems for deep trench latrines

4.0m

1.0m

A

A

2.0m

2.65m deep pit

0.5m

150mm

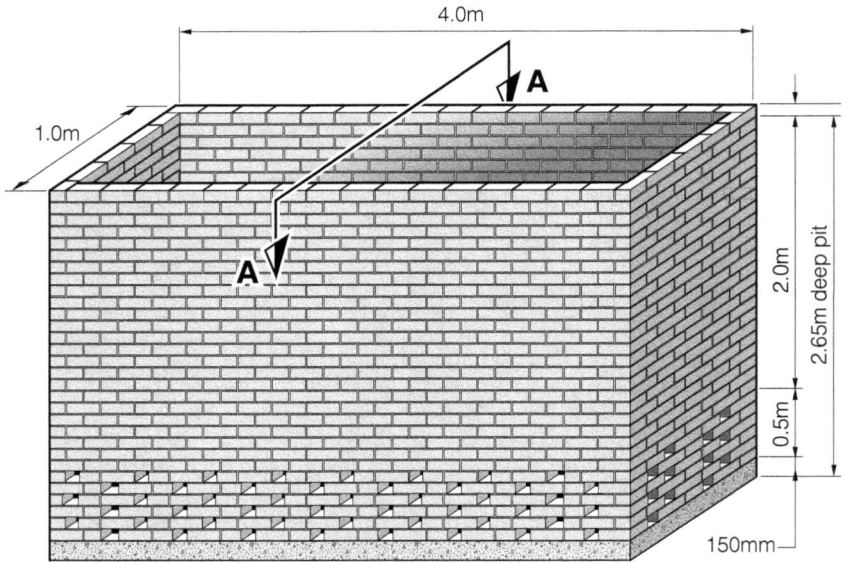

Typical view of brick lining

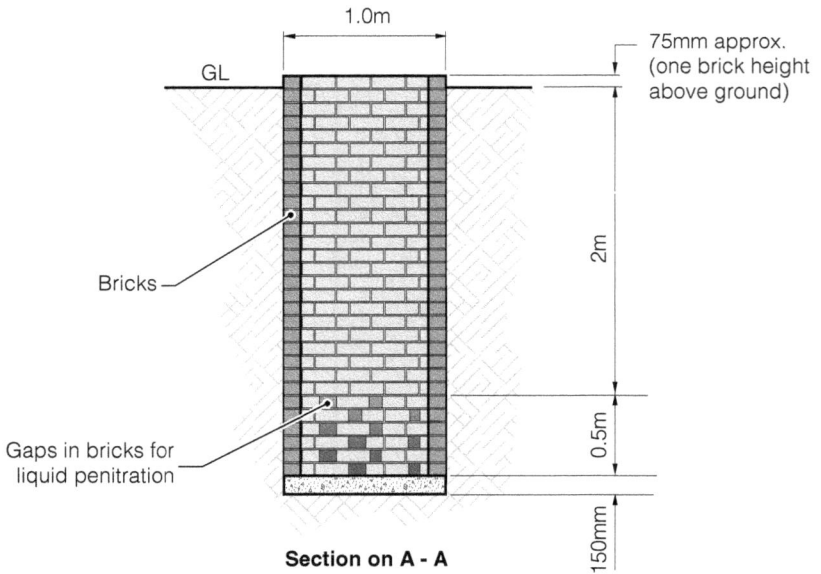

1.0m

GL

75mm approx.
(one brick height
above ground)

Bricks

2m

Gaps in bricks for
liquid penitration

0.5m

150mm

Section on A - A

Figure 7.3. Brick lined pit

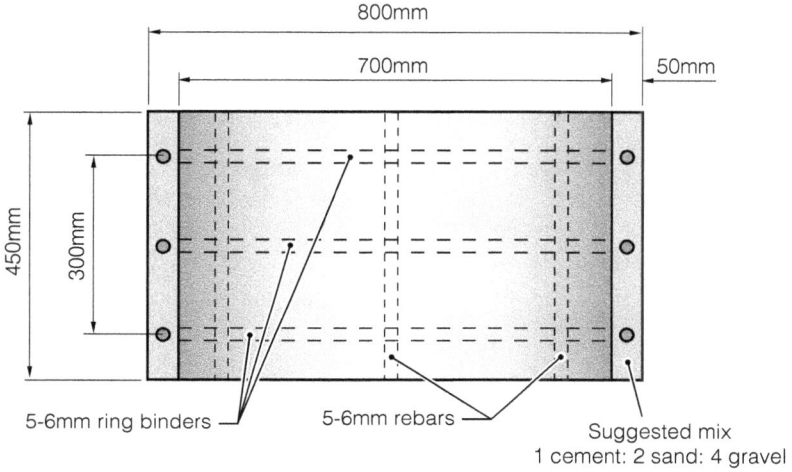

Liner cross-section

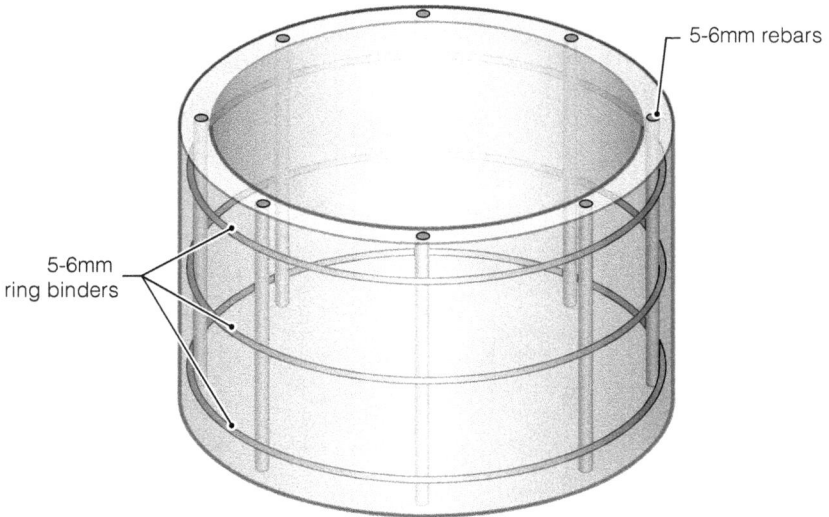

Transparent 3D view to show reinforcement bars

Figure 7.4. Pre-cast concrete ring pit liner

Box 7.2.

Sandbag pit-lining in Kenya and Sudan

Sandbags were used to line pits in unstable soils in refugee and IDP camps in NE Kenya and Sudan. These were found to be cheaper, more durable and more stable than the oil-drum liners used previously.

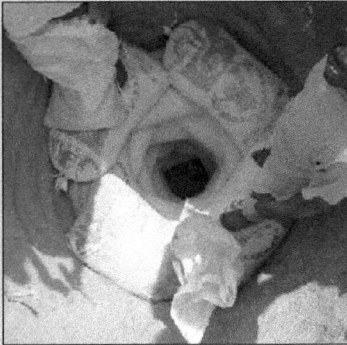

Sandbags are placed within the circular pit with the head-to-tail alignment alternating in each course.

In areas of shallow groundwater, cement was added to the sand mix to increase stability. A dry mix was used when the bags were first filled and a few buckets of water were poured over once the bags were installed in the pit.

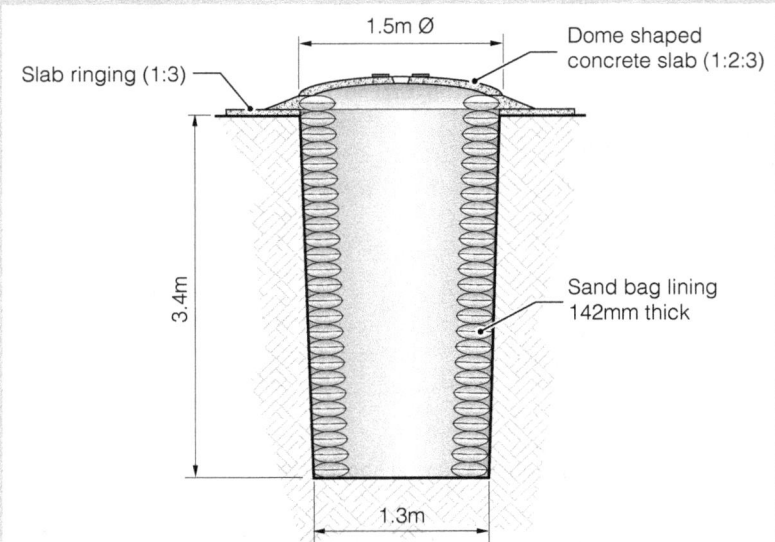

Slab ringing (1:3)

1.5m Ø

Dome shaped concrete slab (1:2:3)

3.4m

Sand bag lining 142mm thick

1.3m

Box 7.3.

Pit-lining with local materials in Mozambique

In Mozambique in response to floods, latrines were built to accommodate affected populations. The latrines were located in an area of sandy soils so the excavated pits had to be lined to ensure that they would not cave in. Baskets woven by local women were evaluated against the other options available, and it was decided that this would be the most viable option for lining the pits. The domed latrine slab was used to cover the pit and other local materials such as grasses and reeds were used to build the superstructure.

The baskets were made out of rigid, dried local grasses (reeds) that are typically used for storing grain. A slightly modified design was first discussed with the women, as a basket with a smaller diameter would accommodate the slab better. Agency staff were able to order a number of baskets and then pick them up. Being rigid and sturdy the sides of the pit did not cave in. It proved to be a relatively cheap solution and was quick to install.

Sizing pits

In order to size pits or tanks it is important to determine the rate at which sludge (including faeces, urine and anal-cleansing material) will accumulate, and the rate at which effluent will infiltrate into the surrounding ground. The top 0.5m of a pit should not be filled; this is to allow safe back-filling and to prevent splashing, unpleasant sights and increased incidence of problems with odour and flies.

The approximate size of the pit in m^3 can be calculated from the following equation:

Volume of pit, V = $\dfrac{(N \times S \times D)}{1000} + 0.5A$ ⇐ **Equation 1**

Where: **N** = number of users

S = sludge accumulation rate (litres/person/year)

D = design life (years)

A = pit-base area (m2)

If the size of the pit is fixed, the time taken to fill it can be calculated by rearranging Equation 1 to find the design life:

Design life, $\quad$ **D =** $\dfrac{(V - 0.5A) \times 1000}{(N \times S)}$

Sludge accumulation rates vary greatly and local figures should be obtained if possible. In the absence of local knowledge, Table 7.4 gives guideline sludge accumulation rates for different wastes and conditions. In many emergency situations, latrines are subjected to heavy use and excreta and anal-cleansing materials are added much faster than the decomposition rate. For this reason the 'normal' sludge rates are increased by 50% for emergency situations.

This method assumes that liquid wastes are absorbed by the surrounding ground. If liquid remains in the pit it will fill much more quickly. This is likely to happen where large volumes of water are used, or where pit walls have a low infiltration capacity. It should also be noted that soil pores become clogged with time, reducing or even stopping infiltration. For this reason, pits should be over-sized rather than under-sized, especially where soil infiltration rates are relatively low.

Table 7.4. Suggested maximum sludge accumulation rates

Wastes deposited and conditions	Sludge accumulation rate 'S' (litres per person per year)	
	Stable situation	Emergency situation
Wastes retained in water where degradable anal-cleansing materials are used	40	60
Wastes retained in water where non-degradable anal-cleansing materials are used	60	90
Wastes retained in dry conditions where degradable anal-cleansing materials are used	60	90
Wastes retained in dry conditions where non-degradable anal- cleansing materials are used	90	135

Source: Franceys et al., 1992

Note: *The term 'wastes retained in water' when applied to a pit latrine means that wastes are in a section of the pit below the water-table*

7.4 Latrine slabs

An important component of a pit latrine is the latrine slab situated above the pit. The purpose of the latrine slab is to cover the top of the pit and, sometimes, provide a surface on which the user puts their feet. The slab should be able to support the weight of a person, easy to clean and should usually be sloped slightly towards the squat-hole to allow liquid to drain. In the early stages of an emergency, many agencies use pre-moulded plastic squatting plates. These are appropriate for immediate rapid implementation and are often suitable for use in emergency trench latrines, health centres, schools and reception centres. For long-term use, however, it is more efficient to use locally manufactured slabs where possible. Slabs can be made of concrete, wood, ferrocement or plastic. Several options with advantages and disadvantages are presented in Table 7.5.

Table 7.5. Comparison of latrine slabs

Slab type	Comments
Oxfam Plastic Slab Size 1.2m x 0.8m	Needs no supporting timbers – just ensure the pit edges are stable and place it on hole. Trench must be no more than 1.0m wide as slab length is 1.2m. Includes foot-operated drop-hole cover. A pour-flush toilet pan can be inserted into the slab for water-washed systems.
Monarflex Plastic Slab Size 0.8m x 0.6m	Not big enough for cubicle alone, normally need to construct platform to place slab on which makes it more expensive and time-consuming than the above option. Hole-covers rapidly go missing.
Wooden Slab	Can be quick if materials available locally, not easy to clean. Prone to termite attack and rotting. Can be covered with plastic sheeting to increase life and ease of cleaning. Not a good long-term solution (deforestation issues).
Bush timber and sticks covered by plastic sheeting and covered with packed earth	Fast and cheap, and can be easily upgraded with a SanPlat concrete slab or plastic slab. Difficult to keep clean, badly affected by rainfall or people washing in the latrine. Wood rots over time.
Dome Slab 1.2m or 1.5m diameter	Needs proper mould, 1 bag of cement (sand and gravel) per slab, no rebar. A good longer-term solution.
SanPlat Slab Size 0.6m x 0.6m	Good for upgrading log/mud slabs. Quick to produce, smaller size, therefore requires less rebar. Can be mass-produced using an all-in-one mould to produce a high-quality, easy-clean surface.
Ferrocement Slabs	Can make slabs thinner, therefore cheaper, than traditional concrete slabs.
Concrete Slab various sizes	Sand, cement and gravel are usually available and easy to make and clean. Requires rebar, which can be difficult & expensive to purchase. Large slabs are not easily transportable.
Plywood Slab	Water-resistant ply is very expensive. Not always easy to purchase.

In societies where people are not used to squatting to defecate, wherever possible toilet pedestals should be used instead of latrine slabs. Locally manufactured pedestals may be available in plastic or wood.

Concrete is usually the preferred material for latrine slabs for second-phase implementation as it is cheap, durable, easy to clean and simple to manufacture. Most concrete slabs are reinforced with steel bars to prevent breaking; reinforcing bars should be placed near the base of the slab to carry the tension forces. The amount of reinforcement will depend on the size of the slab and the load to be carried. Table 7.6 gives suggestions for the **minimum** amount of reinforcement required for different slabs. The last two columns give the preferred spacing of reinforcing bars. Slabs may be rectangular or circular.

Table 7.6. Spacing for steel reinforcing bars in pit-latrine slabs

Slab thickness (mm)	Steel bar diameter (mm)	Spacing of steel bars (mm) in each direction for minimum spans of:				
		1m	1.25m	1.5m	1.75m	2m
65	6	150	150	125	75	50
	8	250	250	200	150	125
80	6	150	150	150	125	75
	8	250	250	250	200	150

The squat-hole in the latrine slab should be large enough to allow defecation and urination without fouling the floor, whilst being small enough for the young and old to span and use in safety. Ideally, this should be a 'keyhole' shape, 160-170mm in diameter and 300-400mm at full length.

Figure 7.5. gives an example of a reinforced concrete latrine slab.

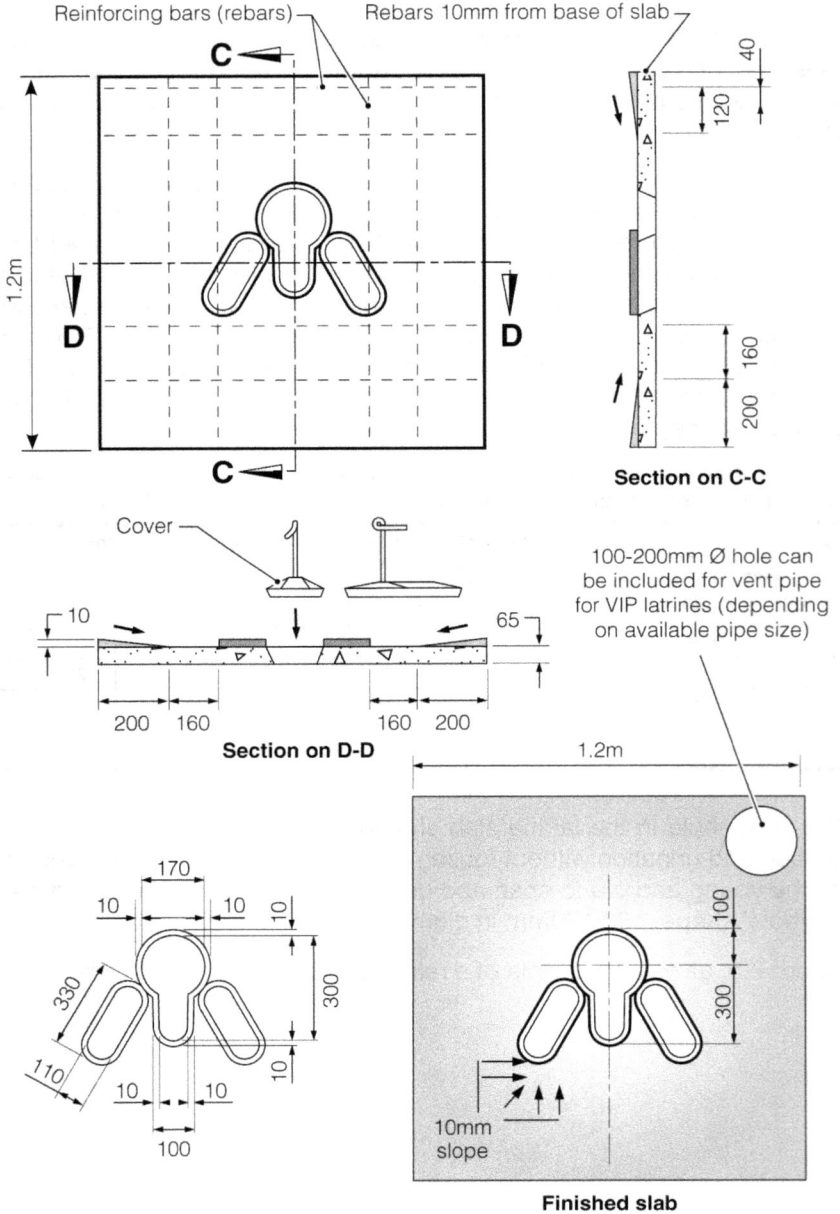

Reinforcing bars (rebars)

Rebars 10mm from base of slab

1.2m

C

D

D

C

40

120

160

200

Section on C-C

Cover

10

65

200   160   160   200

Section on D-D

100-200mm Ø hole can
be included for vent pipe
for VIP latrines (depending
on available pipe size)

170

10   10   10

330

300

110

10   10

100

1.2m

100

300

10mm
slope

Finished slab

Figure 7.5. Reinforced concrete latrine slab

136

Slabs without reinforcement can be made provided the slab is domed. The dome shape causes all the forces in the slab (apart from the rim) to be compressed so reinforcement is not needed. Although not essential, a couple of rounds of steel wire can be embedded in the concrete close to the rim, as this is the only part of the slab under tension. Domed slabs are cheaper than reinforced slabs but more care is required in their manufacture and transport. Such slabs have a typical diameter of 1.2-1.5 metres (see Figure 7.6).

Concrete mixes

Concrete is a mix of cement, sand, gravel (aggregate) and water. Generally, one of the two following design mixes is used:

Cement:	Sand:	Aggregate	
1:	2:	4	*Mix 1*
1:	3:	6	*Mix 2*

Mix 1 will be slightly stronger than Mix 2 due to the increased proportion of cement. In both cases gravel makes up approximately 60% of the volume of concrete. The ratio of water to cement is generally:

Water:	Cement:	
1:	2	*or*
1:	3	

Once the concrete is poured into the mould it must be **compacted** to eliminate voids (air-holes). This can be done manually by using a wooden plank to pound the concrete surface.

The final stage of concrete preparation is **curing** – this simply means keeping the concrete damp while it sets. Concrete can be cured by covering, regular spraying or submerging in water.

The strength and workability of concrete is affected by the:

- concrete mix;
- water/cement ratio; and
- the curing process.

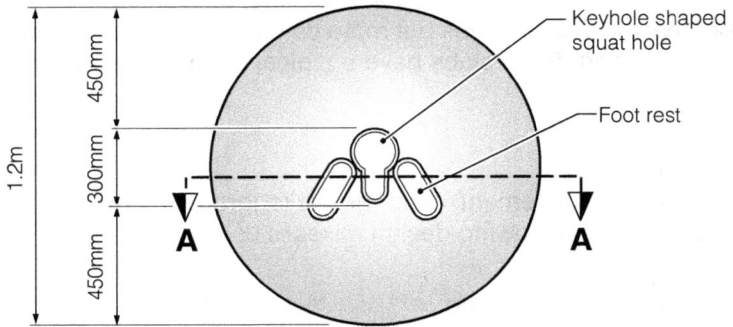

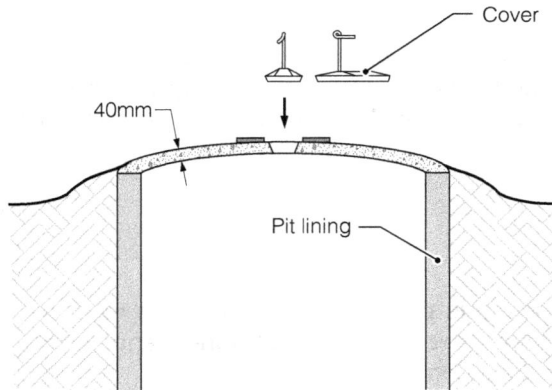

Section on A-A

Figure 7.6. Domed concrete slab (without reinforcement)

Wooden slabs can also be used where concrete is too expensive or is unavailable. Wooden slabs can consist of whole poles covered in mud or soil, or can be sawn-timber platforms (see Figure 7.8). Pits with wooden slabs can be improved by placing a small concrete slab on top to cover the area used for defecation. The slab is quite small (typically 400mm x 600mm) but it covers the area of slab most likely to be fouled. Alternatively, if wooden slabs are to be used, put a thin covering of cement, approximately 25mm thick, on top to facilitate cleaning.

Squat-hole covers

The squat-hole cover for a simple pit latrine is designed to cover the hole when not in use, to minimize flies and odour. A common problem concerning these covers is that they are often not replaced on the hole after use. This may be due to worries of faecal-hand contamination, or may be because covers are taken away for alternative uses.

In some cases, the cover is designed with a long handle, or is tied with a piece of string to the surrounding superstructure. One option is to use a hinged cover which can be opened and closed with the use of an attached piece of string, by hand, or even with the user's foot (see Figure 7.7). The hinges can be made from old tyre rubber, which is available in most situations. The rubber hinges can be attached to the reinforcement within a concrete latrine slab, or tied to the wooden poles of a wooden slab.

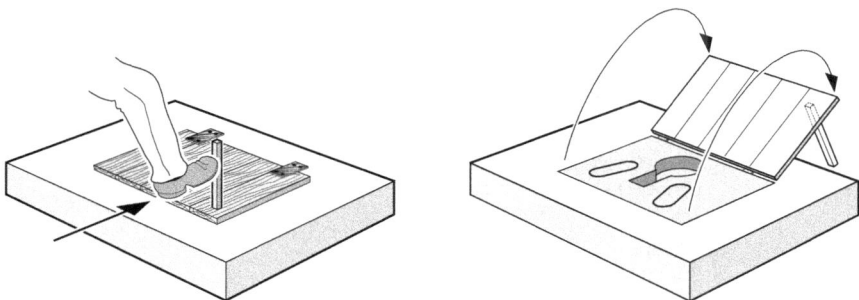

Figure 7.7. Squat-hole cover

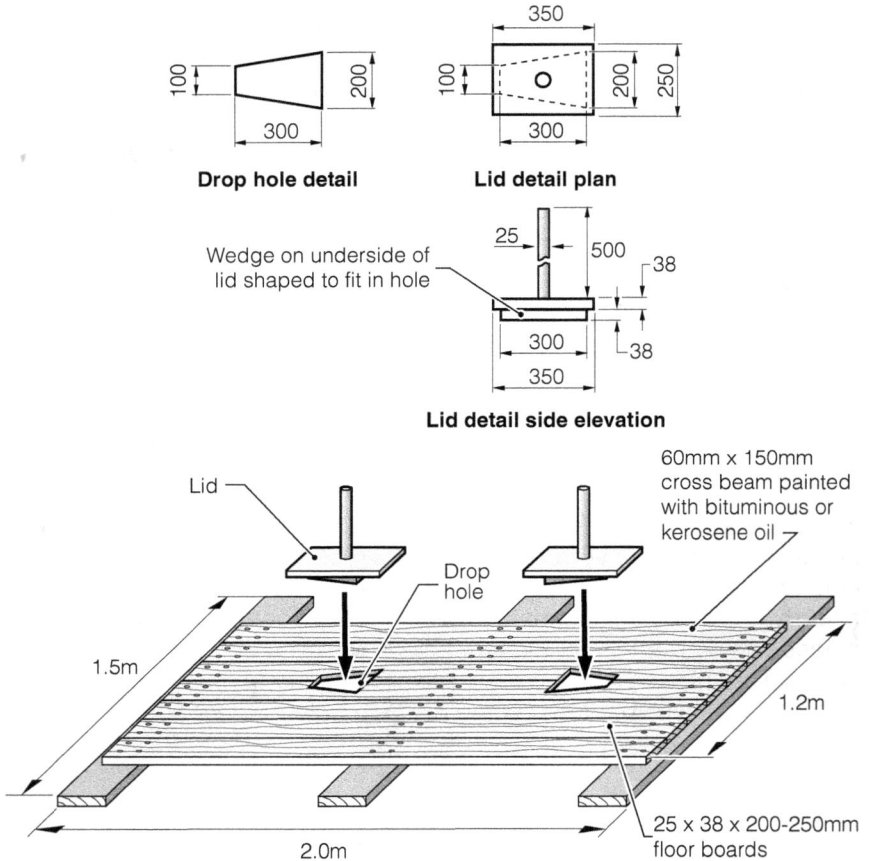

Drop hole detail   **Lid detail plan**

Lid detail side elevation

Timber	Quantity
1 60 x 150 x 1500mm joists across pit	3
2 38 x 200 x 2000mm floor board	6
3 25 x 250 x 350mm lid board	2
4 25mm doa x 500mm lid handle	2
Hardware	
5 75mm tall wire-nails	42
6 Bituminous or kerosene (to render watertight and against termites.	0.5 ltr

Note: Actual dimensions will depend on wooden planks available. Dimensions indicated are suggested minimum values.

Figure 7.8. Wooden slab for twin compartment latrine

7.5　Pour-flush toilet pans

Where people are accustomed to using water-based excreta disposal systems, pour-flush latrines should be installed rather than dry-pit latrines wherever possible.

For immediate emergency use, plastic latrine slabs are also available with built-in pour-flush pans (as pictured below), while there are others which are able to accommodate a pour-flush 'insert' which fits into the normal keyhole-shaped drop-hole.

Photograph 7.1 Plastic pour-flush latrine slab

Locally manufactured pour-flush pans should be used where possible, particularly where these are available in plastic and can be transported easily. Concrete pour-flush pans can also be constructed using appropriate moulds and incorporated into latrine slabs (see Figure 7.9). Where latrines are to discharge wastewater to a septic-tank or sewerage system it is important that pans are compatible with available pipework (commonly ranging from 75mm to 120mm diameter).

Photograph 7.2. Cement pour-flush pan

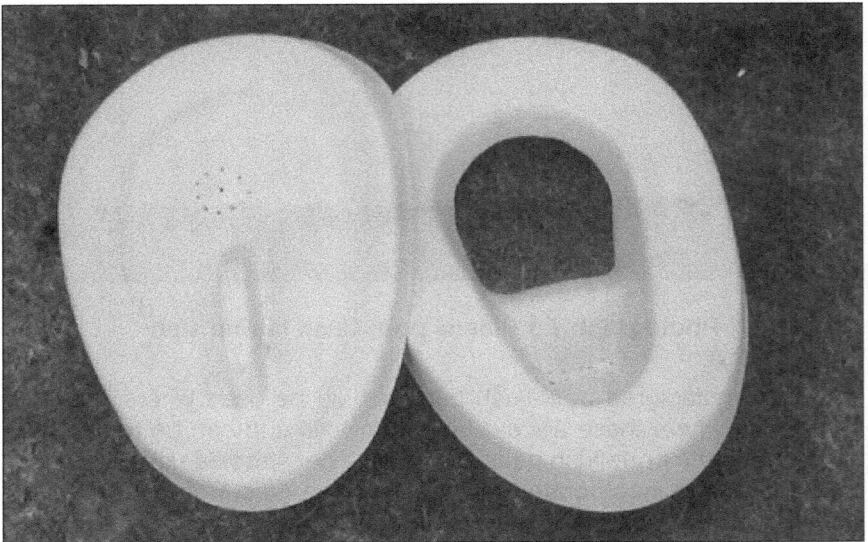

Photograph 7.3. Plastic pour-flush pan and lid

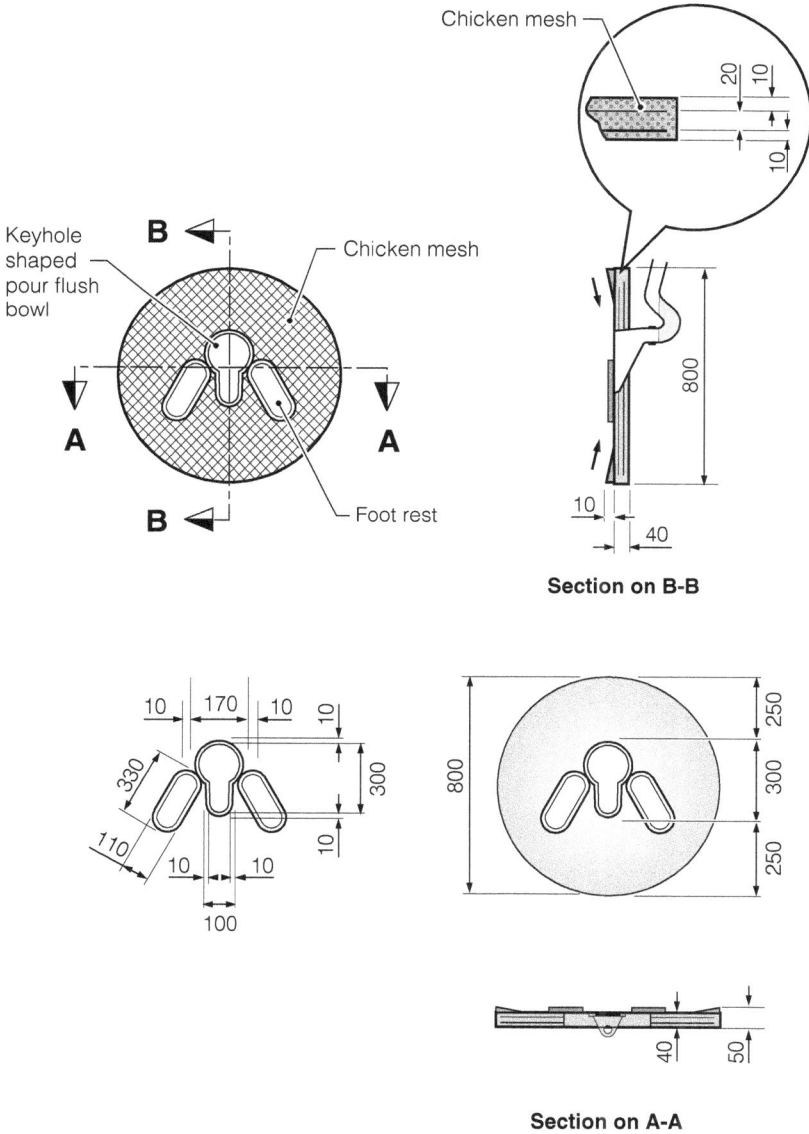

Chicken mesh

20
10
10

Keyhole shaped pour flush bowl

B

Chicken mesh

Foot rest

A   A

B

800

10

40

Section on B-B

10   170   10

10

330

110

10   10

100

300

10

800

250

300

250

40

50

Section on A-A

Figure 7.9. Ferrocement slab with pour-flush bowls
(for use on 800mm ø pre-fab concrete ring)

143

7.6 Superstructure design

To the user, the superstructure is likely to be the most important part of the latrine. For this reason alone, due attention must be given to its design. In some cultures people prefer to defecate in the open and a superstructure may not be required. In general, however, the superstructure must provide the necessary privacy for the comfort and dignity of the users. Materials and techniques used for the superstructure should generally be the same as those used for people's shelters, as this will facilitate ease of construction.

In areas of high rainfall, or for VIP latrines, a roof will be essential, although roofing materials may be stolen where shelter is a priority. In other situations roofs may not be necessary. The superstructure may have a door where desired, or a spiral-shaped entrance can be constructed. The superstructure can, more or less, be of any size and shape that the user desires, although a minimum base area of $1m^2$ is recommended.

Although the superstructure has little direct impact on the health benefits of the latrine (with the possible exception of a VIP latrine), its design is likely to influence whether the latrine will be used and looked after. It is essential, therefore, that the users are involved in the superstructure design, to ensure that it is socio-culturally acceptable and to promote the user's pride in their toilet.

Many superstructure options, using different wall materials, rely on a timber frame (as in Figure 7.10).

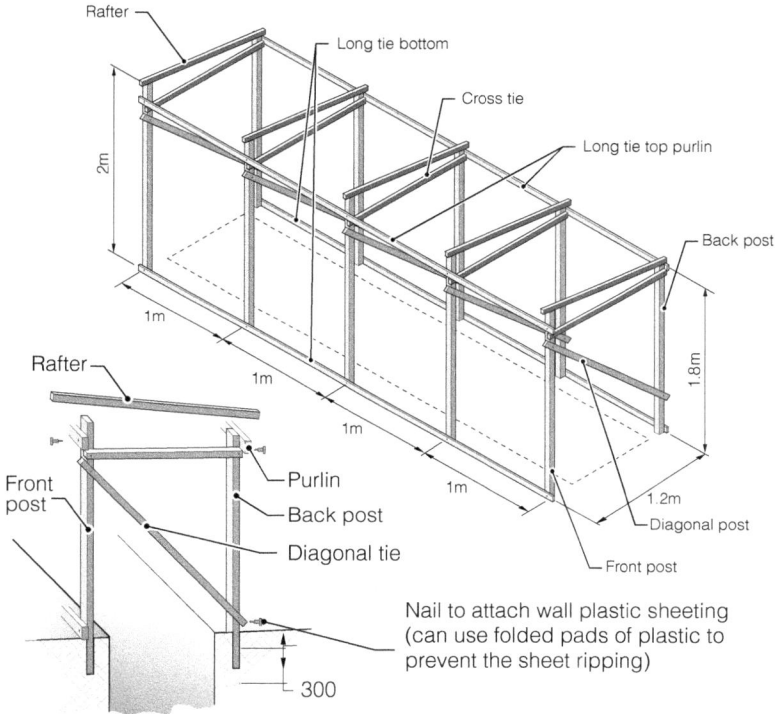

Frame		Quantity
1 Front post	50 x 50 x 2000mm	5
2 Back post	50 x 50 x 1800mm	5
3 Cross tie	25 x 50 x 1200mm	5
4 Diagonal tie	25 x 50 x 1800mm	5
5 Long tie bottom	25 x 75 x 3700mm	2
6 Long tie top	25 x 75 x 4400mm	2
7 Vitall (plastic sheet)	(3700 + 1300) x2 x 1650=	16.5m^2
8 2" (50mm) wirenail	10 x 5	50
9 1" (25mm) bottom pin for wall fixing	250gms	
Roof		
1 Rafter	38 x 50 x 2000mm	5
2 Purlin	25 x 50 x 4400mm	3
3 Roof cover	2000 x 4400mm	8.8m^2
4 2" tin screw		30

Note: Actual dimensions will depend on available timber styles.
Dimensions indicated are suggested minimum values.

Figure 7.10. Timber frame for trench latrine superstructure

Lightweight (portable) superstructures

Where temporary facilities are required, in particular where people are likely to move from one area to another, lightweight superstructures that can be easily disassembled and moved are ideal. One solution is to develop a superstructure frame using PVC piping, which can then be fitted with cloth or plastic sheeting. This approach was used in Burma where refugee migrant workers move around looking for work took their latrines with them!

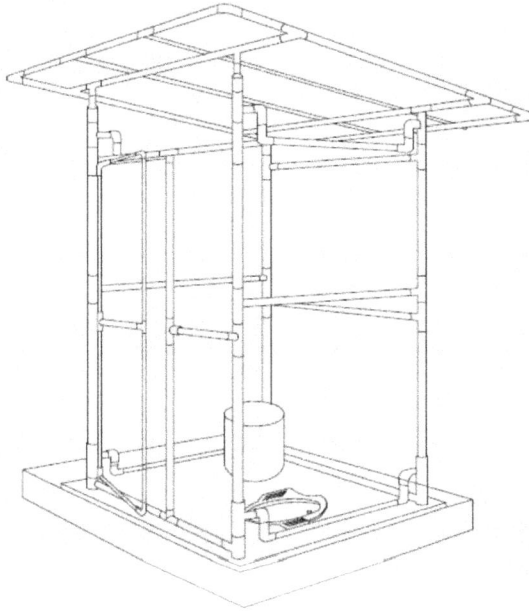

Figure 7.11. PVC-pipe superstructure frame

Superstructures using local materials

Although plastic sheeting is a common option for rapid construction of the superstructure, it often creates a hot, uncomfortable interior, rips easily and can be damaged by strong winds. Where possible, locally available materials should be used. A number of options for latrine superstructure design using local materials are presented in Figures 7.12 and 7.13.

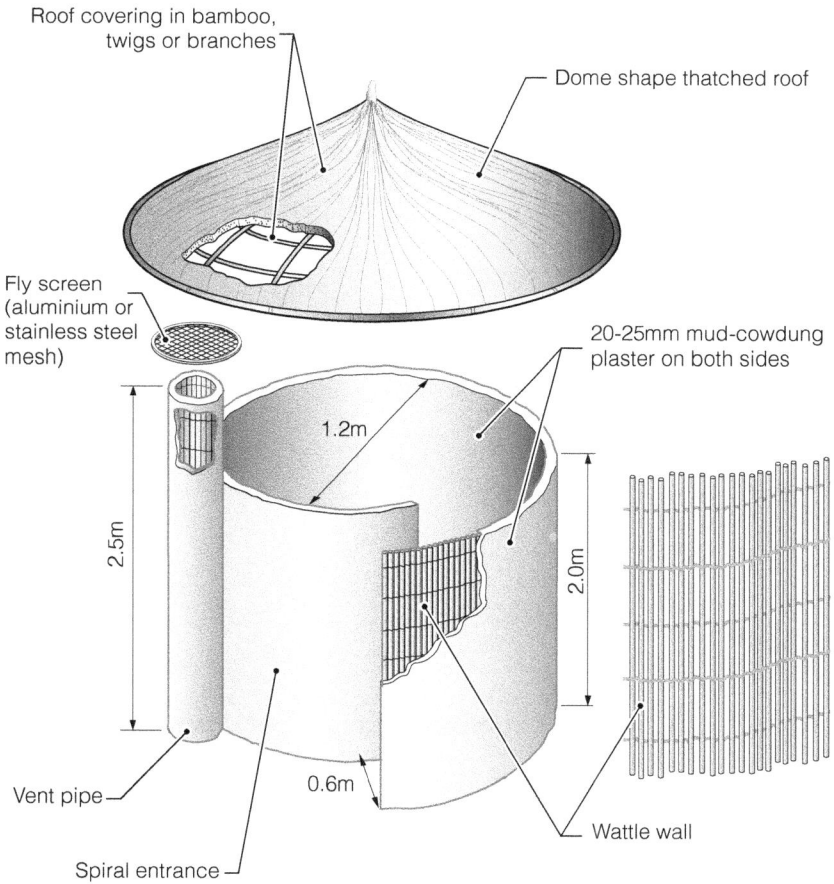

Roof covering in bamboo, twigs or branches

Dome shape thatched roof

Fly screen (aluminium or stainless steel mesh)

20-25mm mud-cowdung plaster on both sides

1.2m

2.5m

2.0m

Vent pipe

0.6m

Spiral entrance

Wattle wall

Note: Approximate dimensions only

**Figure 7.12. Superstructure for family
VIP latrine with spiral entrance**

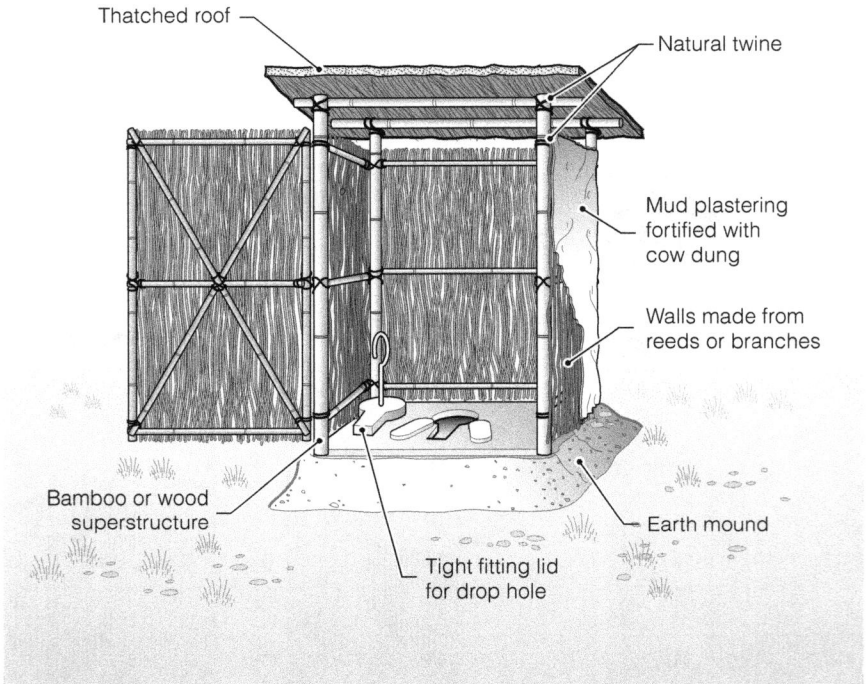

Figure 7.13. Low-cost latrine superstructure

Prefabricated-superstructure units

Unlike latrine slabs, there are few well-designed prefabricated units available for superstructures. Prefabricated-plastic superstructures used in northern Uganda were not liked by many users since they were hot and poorly ventilated. Once they were no longer required they also created a solid-waste problem. Tent-style superstructures have also been developed but these have limited applicability and durability.

The International Federation of Red Cross and Red Crescent Societies (IFRC) has recently developed a plastic superstructure unit that can be deployed for rapid implementation in the immediate stage of an emergency. Each unit can be erected in minutes and, since it is self-supporting, can be installed directly on top of a dug pit. Existing prefabricated latrine slabs (such as the Monarflex) can be fitted directly on to the treated plywood base. Although these units are relatively expensive they may be an appropriate option where facilities need to be installed very rapidly and where there are few local resources available for superstructure construction.

Superstructure design should also consider the need for privacy for menstruation. In Pakistan, combined 'hygiene units' were used for excreta disposal and menstruation-cloth washing and drying (see Box 7.4).

Box 7.4.

Screened hygiene units in Pakistan

Living in close proximity to other people in a camp situation will be a new experience for many people; for women who previously lived in rural areas and in seclusion it will pose additional challenges. As part of the emergency public health response to the Pakistan earthquake of October 2005, screened bathing and toilet units were constructed in some camps. This was felt to be particularly important because many of the women who were living in the camps had previously been living in Purdah (seclusion).

These units consisted of:

- Trench latrines divided into individual units with wooden frames and tarpaulin coverings and doors with simple locks made of binding wire.
- Several individual bathing units which consisted of 20mm (¾") marble slabs sloping towards a stone-filled drain which, in turn, sloped towards a rubble-filled soakpit.

- On top of the soakpit was a metal water container with a tap which was filled daily and was used for handwashing.
- On the side of the handwashing container a sock was tied which included pieces of cut-up soap to encourage the use of soap for washing hands – sometimes the soap went missing, but there were some successes where it remained. It was always the aim that, wherever possible, the handwashing container and soakage pit would be placed next to the exit door to try and encourage people to use the water for handwashing after using the toilet.
- For some units an additional hygiene unit was also included which consisted of a private screened area within the outer screened area. These had a concrete slab with a pipe to a soak-away in which women could wash their menstrual cloths in private. Several washing-lines were also hung across the units and the sides of the units were raised where there was any risk of people looking over and seeing the menstrual cloths hung out to dry.
- The ground within the screened area was covered in broken gravel chippings to prevent mud when it rained and to try and ensure that the units remained hygienic.
- A catchment drain was constructed on the upper side of the units.

Both men's and women's toilet and bathing units were screened and both proved successful. Whilst it was probably more necessary for the women's units to be screened for added privacy, it was also felt to be good practice for the men's units to be screened. The men also faced a lack of privacy in the camps and – if they bathed in the open – this would also lead to added discomfort for the women who either had to go past them or avoid them.

Had the water-availability situation been better and the soakage capacity of the pits and soak-aways been higher, then the screened units could have been expanded to include a tap inside the units, a concrete drainage curtain to a soak-away and, possibly, hot water via a burner unit and some form of drum with tap. An intensive cleaning programme was required to maintain the units. Female cleaners were employed to clean women's units, and male cleaners to clean men's units.

(See next page for design details of the screened units)

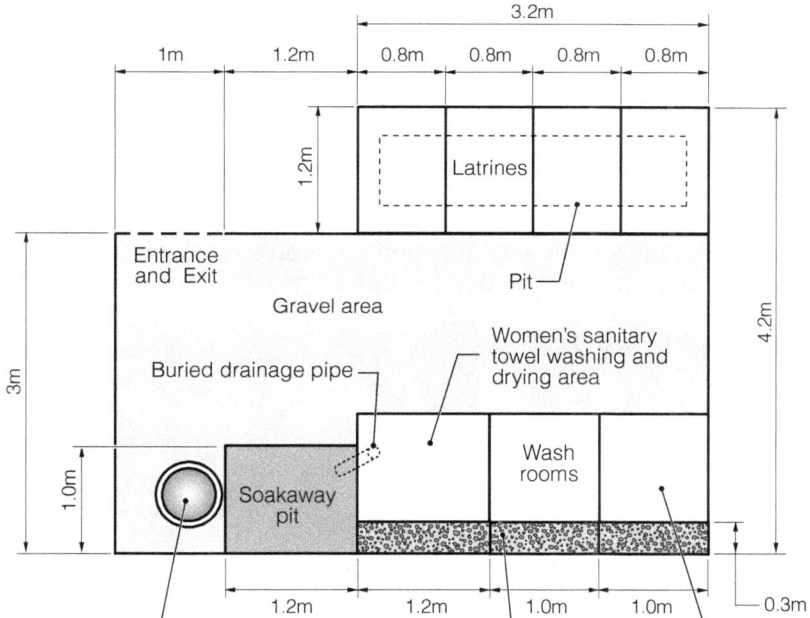

3.2m

1m 1.2m 0.8m 0.8m 0.8m 0.8m

1.2m

Latrines

Entrance
and Exit

Pit

Gravel area

Women's sanitary
towel washing and
drying area

Buried drainage pipe

3m

4.2m

1.0m

Soakaway
pit

Wash
rooms

1.2m 1.2m 1.0m 1.0m └─ 0.3m

Hand-washing barrel with tap and soap
(broken into pieces to try and prevent it
being stolen, and hung in a sock or small
sack tied to the hand washing barrel).

The barrel should ideally be standing on
the soak-pit and near to the exit door of the
screened areas (as a reminder for people
to wash their hands).

Stone filled drainage
channel which should
be within the wash room
units and under the covered
roof area.

Sloping concrete or
marble slabs placed on
a bed of sand, with smooth
finish for easy cleaning.

See **Appendix 4.8** for the relevant bill of quantities.

Figure 7.14. Women's latrine/washroom screened units for camps

151

The need to consider access for disabled people is also important when designing latrine superstructures (see Box 7.5).

Box 7.5.

Designing for disabled people in Pakistan

In Pakistan – in response to the October 2005 earthquake – selected trench latrine cubicles were doubled in size to allow for wheelchair access and, later, a commode chair was placed over the squat-holes. Bedpans were also provided for people who were immobile and unable to leave their beds to use the toilet.

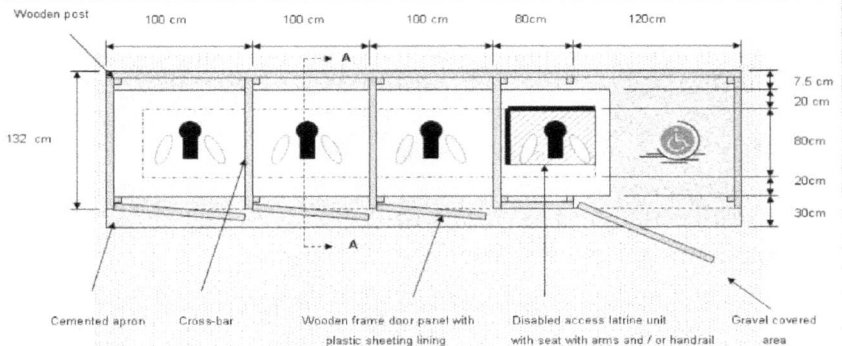

Superstructures must be locally appropriate and, where traditional emergency facilities are not acceptable, it may be necessary to seek non-traditional solutions through consultation with the intended users and local artisans (see Box 7.6).

Box 7.6.

Bathing and latrine facilities after the Bam earthquake in Iran

Following the Bam earthquake in December 2003, in the initial emergency phase aid agencies implemented shallow-pit latrines and communal trench latrines but these were not widely accepted. There was, therefore, a need to find a more acceptable longer-term option.

The local custom in Bam was to construct two pour-flush latrines per house, one inside and the other in the courtyard, both connected to deep unlined pits – with an average pit depth of 20m. So the agencies decided that the quick but long-lasting solution would be to provide appropriate portable superstructures for the outside latrines, which could be recovered and cleaned from the rubble in the family courtyards.

They called for a joint tender to design and construct an appropriate superstructure locally. Several options were presented, using materials such as fibreglass, canvas and galvanised iron, but the selected design was an aluminium cabin. Over the course of two months 234 aluminium cabins were installed as toilets; users were very satisfied with the design, which was also approved by Government. The decision to fabricate the cabins locally in Bam acted as a big booster for the revival of the local economy, and helped build the capacity and skills of local artisans.

7.7 Septic-tank design

For septic-tanks to function properly it is essential that they are designed and operated correctly. The design stages for a septic-tank are outlined below:

1. **Choose a suitable location** – this should be downhill from the source of sewage, *at least* 30m from the nearest water supply and at least 3m from the nearest building. Avoid areas where rainwater would stand or flow over the tank or vehicles could drive over it. (Draw a plan showing the septic-tank and distances to dwellings, property lines, wells, water sources and any other prominent man-made or natural features. Show the ground slope. See Figure 7.18.)

2. **Calculate volume of wastewater to be treated per day** – this can be determined by estimating toilet visits per day and water used per flush. If the quantity of water supplied to the toilet block or institution to be served is known then the daily wastewater flow can be taken as 90% of daily water supply. This should be monitored where possible, before and after construction, as an increase in wastewater flow (such as a result of additional sullage) will affect the retention time and may mean that the septic-tank does not function properly.

3. **Decide on a retention time (R)** – this is based on daily wastewater flow and can be determined from Table 7.7.

Table 7.7. Recommended septic-tank retention times

Daily wastewater flow	Retention time 'R' (hours)
Less than 6m^3	24
Between 6 and 14m^3	33 – 1.5Q
Greater than 14m^3	12

4. **Determine tank volume (T)** using the following equation:

$$\textbf{Total tank volume (T)} = \textbf{clear-liquid retention volume (A)} + \textbf{sludge and scum volume (B)} + \textbf{ventilation space (V)}$$

A = Q x R/24

Where: **A** = liquid retention volume (m³)

          Q = volume of wastewater treated per day (m³)

          R = tank retention time (hours)

B = P x N x S x F

Where: **P** = Number of people using the system

          B = sludge storage capacity in litres

          N = the number of years between sludge emptying

          S = rate of sludge and scum accumulation

(S = 25 litres per person per year for tanks receiving WC waste only, and 40 litres per person per year for tanks receiving WC waste and sullage. As a rule of thumb, two thirds of storage volume is for sludge and a third for scum.)

          F = Sludge-digestion factor (see Table 7.8)

Table 7.8. Sludge-digestion factors 'F'

Years between desludging	Average air temperature		
	Greater than 20°C all year	**Between 10°C and 20°C all year**	**Less than 10°C in winter**
1	1.3	1.15	2.5
2	1.0	1.15	1.5
3	1.0	1.0	1.27
4	1.0	1.0	1.15
5	1.0	1.0	1.06
6 or more	1.0	1.0	1.0

Ventilation volume (V) is the volume of air space required between the top of the liquid and the base of the cover. This should be a depth of 300mm, hence the volume will depend on the tank dimensions.

The tank should be divided into two compartments, the first of which should be twice as long as the second. The total length should be approximately three times the width, W. The tank depth should be at least 1.2m and, ideally, 1.5m. It should not exceed three times the width.

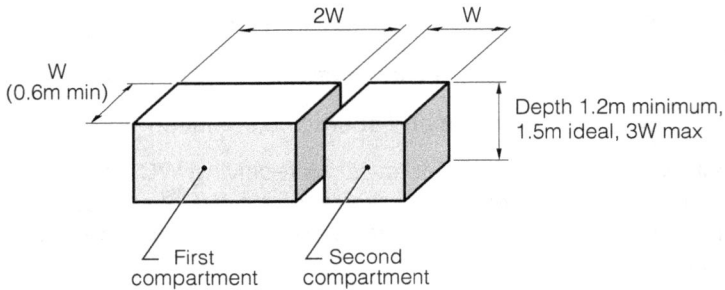

Figure 7.15. Basic tank dimensions

For a tank depth of 1.5m the required width, W can be found from:

$$W = \sqrt{\frac{A + B}{3.6}}$$

Note: This equation can be used only for a depth of 1.5m (with a vent space of 300mm) and if the tank length is equal to 3W.

If the calculated value of W is less than 0.6m, then 0.6m should be used instead.

Septic-tank construction
The walls of the tank can be made of poured, reinforced concrete, stone masonry, brick or concrete blocks. The tank should be made water-tight with a 25mm coating of cement plaster, applied in two coats, in order to avoid infiltration around the tank and maintain an anaerobic space. The

base should be at least 150mm thick and should be reinforced (except for very small tanks). The roof of the tank can be made of removable sections with lifting handles (for easy access) or a solid, reinforced concrete roof with round access holes (minimum diameter 0.6m). These provide access to the tank for desludging, checking wastewater levels and maintenance. If the tank will be below the groundwater level at any time the weight of the empty tank should be greater than the weight of water displaced, otherwise the tank may float (see Section 6.1).

Inlet and outlet pipes consist of 'T' pipes. On the outlet this is to avoid scum or solids going into the soakfield. On the inlet this is to reduce turbulence. The base of the tank can slope down towards the inlet in a large tank to allow more sludge to be stored at the inlet end. The outlet on a larger tank can be a weir design. The inlet wastewater pipe should be ventilated above head height in order to allow the gases produced in the tank to escape.

See Figure 7.16 for septic-tank design details and **Appendix 4.9** for a bill of quantities for a septic-tank.

Soakfield design

The effluent from a septic-tank still contains pathogens and must be disposed of into a sewerage system or alternative disposal system such as a reed-bed, soakpit or soakfield (infiltration field). A soakfield consists of a series of 15-30m long trenches with open-jointed **100mm diameter** pipes laid on rocks, broken bricks or gravel.

The top of the pipe should be laid about 50mm under a layer of building paper/straw (see Figure 7.17). The bottom of the trench should be at least 1.5m above the water-table and have a minimum slope of 2%. Pipes can be made porous by making them out of concrete without sand, not sealing the joints or, in the case of plastic pipes, cutting slots or holes in them (at least 6mm in diameter).

The trenches should be narrow (0.3-1.0m) and deep (1.5-2.0m) and arranged in series so that each trench overflows into the next one. Trenches should be approximately 2m apart. The length of the trench can be calculated using the formula below:

$$\text{Length (m)} = \frac{\text{number of users x wastewater flow (l/person/day)}}{2 \times \text{effective depth (m)} \times \text{infiltration rate (l/m}^2\text{/day)}}$$

157

10mm vertical reinforced bars

From toilet

Soak-away

1.5m

3.0m

1.5m

A

A

10mm horizontal binder

110mm Ø uPVC effluent pipe

Plan of septic-tank

Scum — Liquid level — Lifting hook

at least 75mm — Footstep — 1/2 Block

at least 25mm — B

GL

560mm or 40% (Id)

Minimum 1.0mØ

From toilet

1.7m

300mm

600mm

200mm

600mm

150mm

280mm or 20% liquid depth (Id)

Sludge

B

10mm reinforced bar

Mixed stone or brick bats

Sand/soil

3.0m depth or deeper where possible

Slaughtered pipe

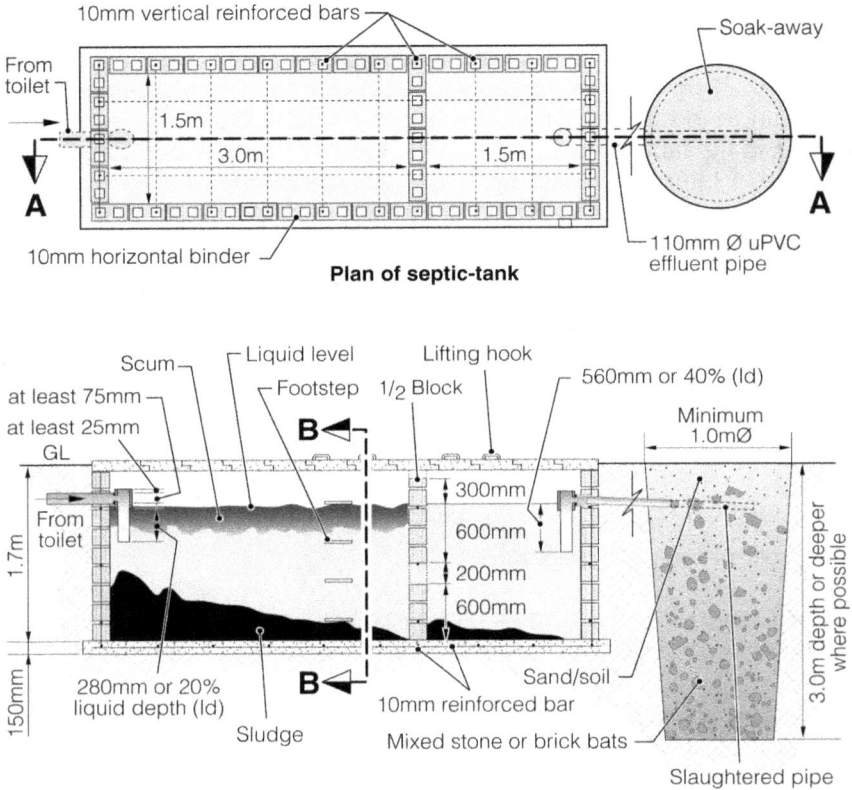

Section on A-A reinforced in unstable soil

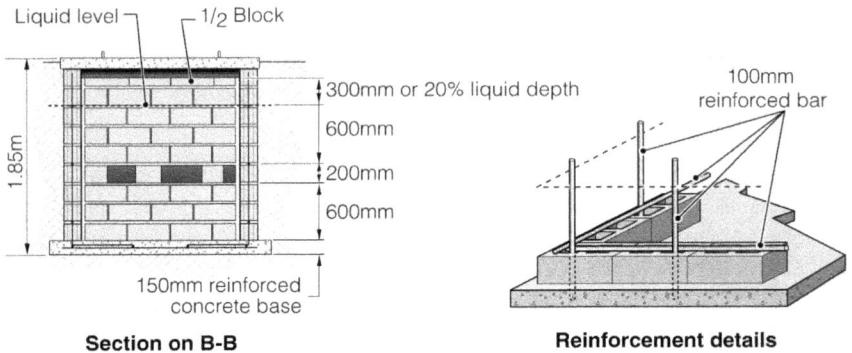

Liquid level — 1/2 Block

1.85m

300mm or 20% liquid depth

600mm

200mm

600mm

150mm reinforced concrete base

Section on B-B

100mm reinforced bar

Reinforcement details

Figure 7.16. Septic-tank design

158

The infiltration rate can be estimated from Table 7.9.

Table 7.9. Suggested infiltration rates

Type of soil	Infiltration rate (l/m²/day)
Coarse / medium sand	50
Fine sand, loamy sand	33
Sandy loam, loam	25
Porous silty clay / porous silty clay loam	20
Compact silty loam, compact silty clay loam and non-expansive clay	10
Expansive clay	<10

Regular monitoring is required – if the septic-tank is not functioning properly solids may enter and block the infiltration pipes.

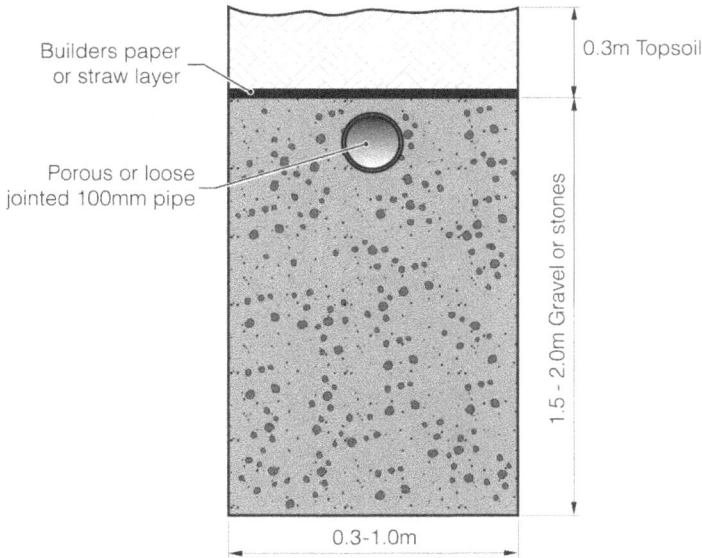

Figure 7.17. Soakfield trench

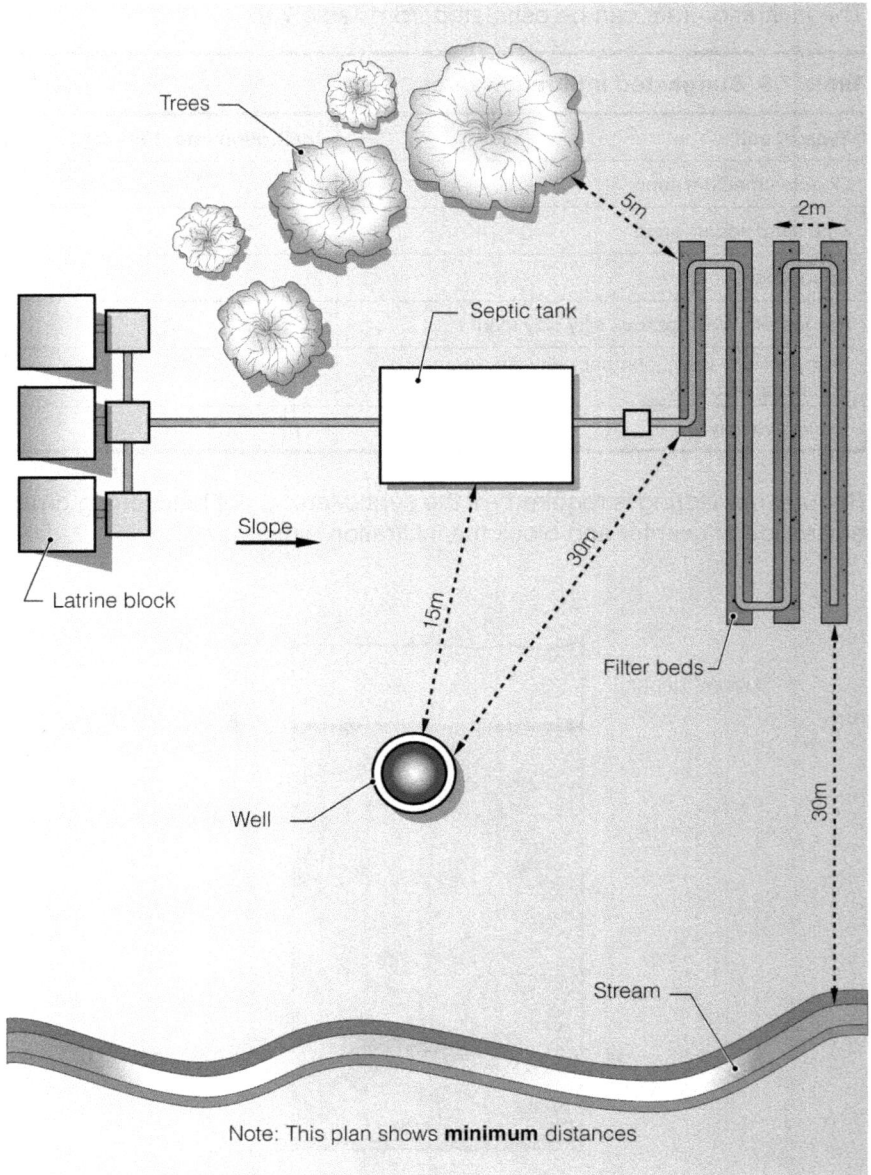

Trees

5m

2m

Septic tank

Slope →

Latrine block

15m

30m

Filter beds

Well

30m

Stream

Note: This plan shows **minimum** distances

Figure 7.18. Septic-tank location plan

8.
Operation and Maintenance

This chapter provides guidance on the effective operation and maintenance of excreta disposal facilities.

8.1 Public health promotion

Any excreta disposal programme must include the promotion of public health. This means that communities must be mobilized to promote appropriate hygiene practices related to the design, use and maintenance of facilities.

A number of studies have suggested that the impact of hygiene practices on sanitation-related disease could be as great as that of the actual provision of sanitation facilities. Public health and hygiene promotion is widely believed to be one of the most effective means we have to reduce the toll of diarrhoeal diseases. It can also be an effective way to encourage participation and empower communities. Public health promotion in relation to excreta disposal should focus on:

- the appropriate use and maintenance of excreta disposal facilities;
- the safe disposal of faeces (especially those of children);
- handwashing after defecation and prior to food preparation;
- the use and safe disposal of appropriate anal-cleansing material;
- the control of flies and other insect vectors.

Practitioners should keep to the following seven principles of hygiene promotion (from Curtis, 1999):

1. Target a small number of risk practices – from the viewpoint of controlling diarrhoeal disease, the priorities for hygiene-behaviour change are likely to include handwashing with soap (or a local substitute) after contact with faeces, and the safe disposal of adults' and children's faeces.

2. Target specific audiences – these may include mothers, children, older siblings, fathers, opinion leaders, or other groups. One needs to identify who is involved in childcare, and who influences them or takes decisions for them.

3. Identify the motives for changed behaviour – these motives often have nothing to do with health. People may be persuaded to wash their hands so that their neighbours will respect them, so that their hands smell nice, or for other motives. By working with the target groups, one can discover their views of the benefits of the safer hygiene practices. This provides the basis for a motivational strategy.

4. Hygiene messages need to be positive – people learn best when they laugh, and will listen for a long time if they are entertained. Programmes which attempt to frighten their audience will alienate them. There should be no mention, therefore, of doctors, death or diarrhoea in hygiene promotion programmes.

   The only exception to this is an acute epidemic-related emergency, such as a cholera outbreak, when a more directive approach may be necessary, whereby people are informed of the disease risks and transmission routes, and are made aware of the key practices required to tackle these.

5. Identify appropriate channels of communication – we need to understand how the target audiences communicate. For example, what proportion of each listens to the radio, attends social or religious functions, or goes to the cinema? Traditional and existing channels are easier to use than setting up new ones, but they can only be used effectively if their nature and capacity to reach people are understood.

6. Decide on a cost-effective mix of channels – several channels giving the same messages can reinforce one another. There is always a trade-off between reach, effectiveness and cost. Mass media reach many people cheaply, but their messages are soon forgotten. Face-to-face communication can be highly effective in encouraging behaviour change, but tends to be very expensive per capita.

7. Hygiene promotion needs to be carefully planned, executed, monitored and evaluated – at a minimum, information is required at regular intervals on the outputs (e.g. how many broadcasts, house visits, etc.), and the population coverage achieved (e.g. what proportion of target audiences heard a broadcast?). Finally, indicators of the impact on the target behaviours must be collected and fed into the planning process.

For more detailed information on hygiene promotion, refer to Ferron, Morgan & O'Reilly (2006) *Hygiene Promotion: From relief to development*. Intermediate Technology Development Group Publications: UK.

8.2 Cleaning and maintenance

The cleaning and maintenance of excreta disposal facilities, especially communal latrines, is often the single biggest problem faced in promoting their use. Put simply, **if latrines are not clean, people will not use them**. Latrines should be cleaned daily to prevent disease transmission through contact with faeces and flies and, perhaps more crucially, to prevent insanitary conditions and odour which may deter people from using them.

Individual families should be responsible for their own units but, where there are communal facilities, special arrangements must be made to keep them clean. Members of the affected community can usually be effectively employed through paid work or other incentives to undertake these tasks with proper supervision, equipment and training. Education should also be provided to the wider community to ensure that people are aware of the importance of using provided sanitation facilities and the uptake of corresponding hygiene practices, such as handwashing. Where there are latrines at health centres, particular attention should be paid to their maintenance and cleanliness as patients are likely to be more susceptible to disease.

Even where latrines are not particularly well-designed and there are no lids on drop-holes, thorough cleaning and maintenance are the key measures in reducing odour and flies. When cleaning latrines, disinfectants such as chlorine can be used to clean squatting-plates but should **not** be poured into pit latrines or tanks as this inhibits the natural biological degradation of the excreta. Public health promotion activities are crucially important to mobilize communities to promote and ensure the cleanliness of latrines.

Although thorough cleaning can go a long way towards controlling and reducing flies or smells, it is generally accepted that most latrines will attract some level of these. Pit latrines should be at least 6 metres away from shelters and other buildings to minimize the effects of odour, flies and pests from bothering or harming the population (UNHCR, 2000).

Some key issues to consider when implementing latrine-cleaning programmes are presented below:

- Where latrines belong to individual families or are shared by two to four families it is generally easy to encourage them to clean and maintain their own latrines (responsibility rotating between families weekly).

- Where communal facilities are in place (i.e. shared by more than four families) it is almost always necessary to employ some members of the affected community to clean and maintain latrines; this provides employment and helps to avoid conflict between community members.

- Co-ordination with other agencies working in the same area is important to ensure that a consistent approach is adopted, if people in one location are paid for O&M and people in another location are expected to perform the same tasks on a purely voluntary basis this is likely to create unrest.

- For large sites, such as large camps, the sheer volume of work required for appropriate O&M is huge. This makes the scale of supervision difficult and it is important that community members are empowered to manage this wherever possible.

- The quantity of equipment required for cleaning (disinfectants, mops, rags etc.) may also be considerable and an appropriate distribution system must be developed. This is commonly implemented in conjunction with a hygiene promotion programme.

8.3 Handwashing

Many studies have been conducted demonstrating the importance of handwashing with soap as an important means of reducing the risk of diarrhoeal disease in regular development and during emergencies as a means of improving public health conditions. Studies generally indicate that washing hands with soap can reduce the risk of diarrhoeal disease by 42-47% (Curtis and Cairncross, 2003); while a study in a refugee camp in Malawi indicated that the presence of soap in a household led to a reduction of 27% of diarrhoeal episodes (Peterson et al., 1998).

Because diarrhoeal diseases are of faecal origin, interventions are needed which prevent faecal material from entering the domestic environment. The key primary barriers to the transmission of enteric pathogens are safe stool-disposal and adequate handwashing, especially after contact with faecal materials during anal-cleansing of adults and children.

If diarrhoea is a major problem – with evidence or risk of high morbidity or mortality (and it often is) – the focus of response should be excreta disposal, handwashing, protection of water from contamination and the provision of clean water in adequate quantities. The necessary software or promotional interventions should similarly focus intensively on these aspects until the risks have been mitigated.

Handwashing with soap (or ash if soap is not available) should be promoted at three key times: after defecation; after cleaning child excreta and before eating or preparing a meal.

Excreta disposal facilities should, wherever possible, be accompanied by appropriate handwashing facilities. The task of handwashing is an ambiguous and awkward activity simply because one's hands must be used for the task of washing one's hands. A number of appropriate technical solutions have been used in the past to make handwashing easier, more convenient and more accessible.

These solutions include the following:

- The preferred option is to have a tap near each latrine connected to a piped water system.

- Miscellaneous containers with taps fitted to them (see Figures 8.1 and 8.2).

- Small leaking containers fitted with a handle. The leaky container is used to provide water sparingly by dipping it into a body of water and hanging it up. The water then drizzles out through a small hole in the bottom over a person's hands.

- The 'Tippy Tap' (Cairncross and Curtis, 2003) has been one of the more well-known and popular designs from the viewpoint of the development worker. The Tippy Tap is made from an old cooking container or similar that is suspended. It allows water to flow into a spout when it is tipped upright and drizzle out through a small hole in the end of the spout onto the hands (see Figure 8.3).

- The 'Handy Andy' is a small plastic device which is fitted into a reservoir or container and works by releasing water in small amounts when the user pushes up the plastic pin in the bottom (see Figure 8.3).

- The handwashing dispenser unit is a plastic moulded device designed and developed in South Africa. It screws onto a plastic drinking-bottle filled with water. The bottle is then turned upright and fits into a wall bracket ready to dispense small amounts of water when an inverted plunger is lifted.

- The 'Captap' (Harries, 2004) is a spring-loaded device that fits into the cap of a jerrycan. You dispense water through the centre of the cap by moving the handle, up or down. The Captap stems the flow of water by using a rubber seal that is pulled against the inside of the cap under the tension of the spring. The seal is made out of a bicycle or car-tyre tube (see Figure 8.3).

Photograph 8.1. The 'Captap' in use in Liberia

Drum with tap

Tap

Oxfam bucket

Soap (can be attached to stand by a string)

Mixed gravel soakaway pit

Overflow channel

Surface drainage channel

Overflow channel
300mm deep x 200mm wide

500

500

1000

Mixed gravel or brick bats for soakaway back-fill

Drainage channel connected to surface drain

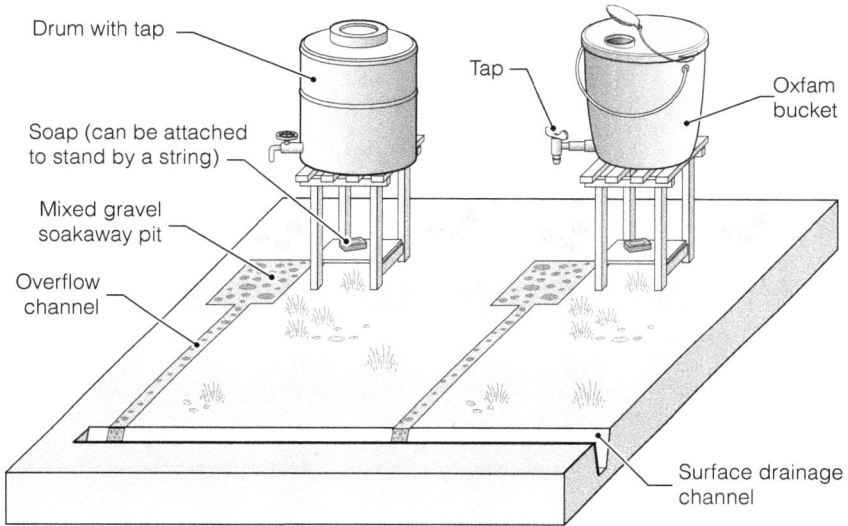

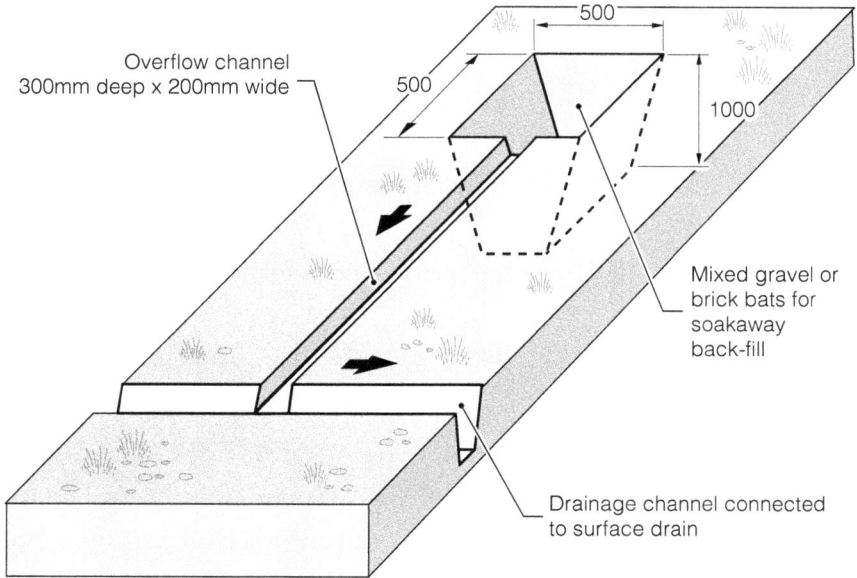

Soakaway detail

Figure 8.1. Traditional handwashing devices

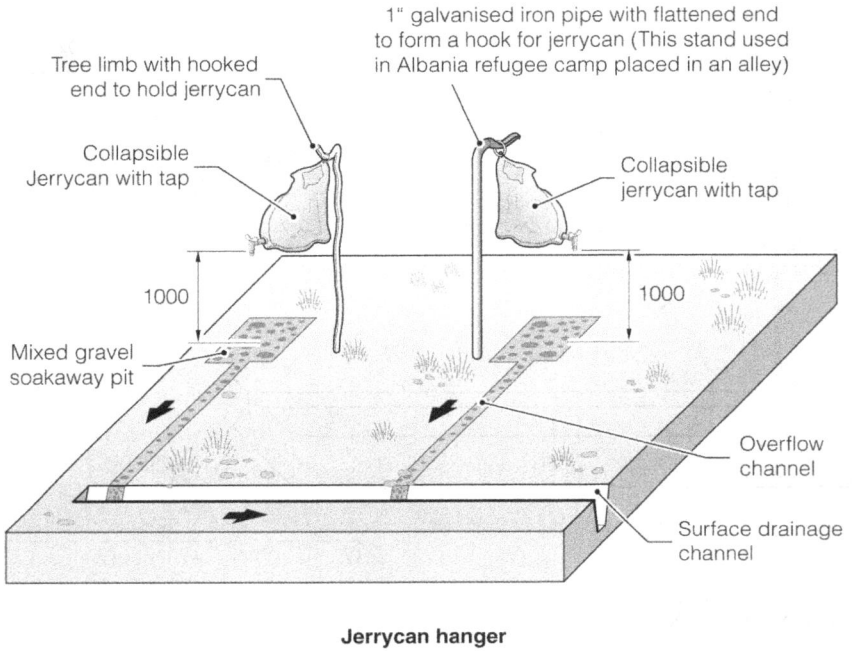

Jerrycan hanger

Figure 8.2. Traditional handwashing devices

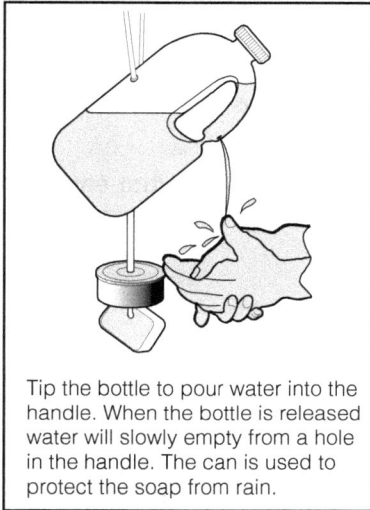

Tip the bottle to pour water into the handle. When the bottle is released water will slowly empty from a hole in the handle. The can is used to protect the soap from rain.

The Tippy Tap

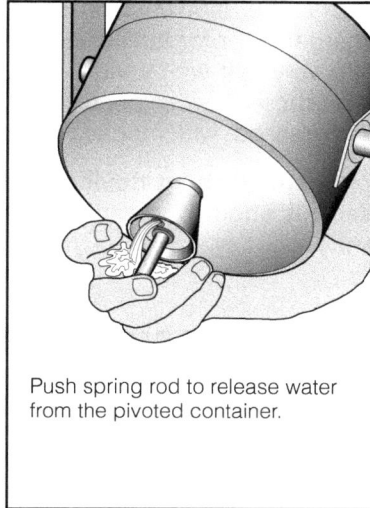

Push spring rod to release water from the pivoted container.

The Handy Andy

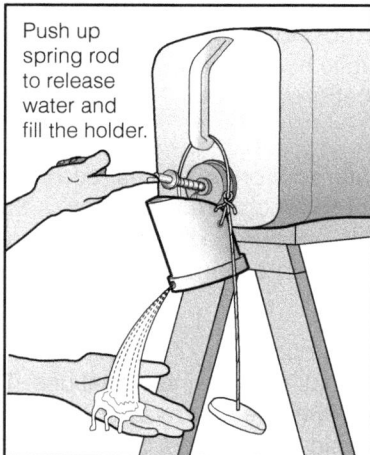

Push up spring rod to release water and fill the holder.

The Captap - Stage 1

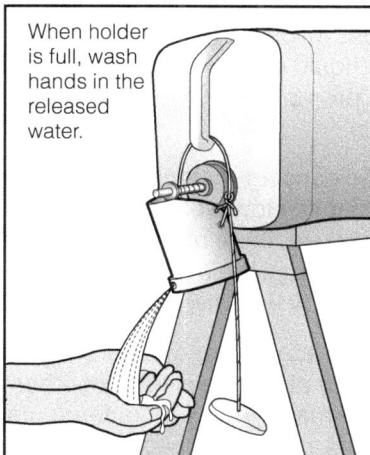

When holder is full, wash hands in the released water.

The Captap - Stage 2

Figure 8.3. Improved handwashing devices

In general, the handwashing options illustrated are for the 1st phase of an emergency or for family use. Heavy use may cause soakaway pits to clog up very fast with sand and soap and produce unpleasant odours. Because these devices contain only small volumes of water they must be regularly refilled, which poses a significant O&M issue.

Simple handwashing devices may be used in the initial emergency phase, but should be replaced by taps close to toilets as soon as possible.

8.4   Anal-cleansing material

Arrangements must be made to assure the availability of appropriate anal-cleansing materials at or near all latrines, and an appropriate method of disposal if necessary, as this is essential for hygiene. All people use some form of anal-cleansing material and it should not be assumed that the population will have their own supply. In the initial phase of an emergency it is essential that the affected community is consulted to determine the preferred and current methods of anal-cleansing. This is important to determine what facilities are appropriate and what measures need to be put in place (see Box 8.1). Where possible, the consultation process should occur in conjunction with public health promoters who should also promote handwashing after defecation and after handling infants' stools.

Anal-cleansing materials range from water to stones, leaves, corn husks and paper. However, while it is important to recognize what people traditionally use, there may also be the need to encourage people to use more available materials such as paper or water, in a densely populated site affected by an emergency.

Where water is used for anal-cleansing, a container of water should be supplied at or in facilities, together with small pots for individual use. This can be managed by the attendants along with the handwashing facilities. If this is not done, people may use plastic bottles and drop these into latrines making them inoperable.

Where solids are used, the appropriate material may also need to be provided. If biodegradable objects, such as corn cobs, are used it may be acceptable to drop these into latrines but these will cause pit latrines to fill up faster. Where space is limited or water-based sanitation systems are in place it may be necessary to provide receptacles to collect soiled material. These materials should then be buried or burned and not deposited where they will create a health hazard.

Box 8.1.

Anal-cleansing in Afghanistan

In response to IDPs affected by severe drought conditions and the effects of civil war in Panjshir Valley, Afghanistan a hygiene-promotion programme commenced. Immediately there were reports of problems with anal-cleansing, particularly for children. Affected populations were apparently finding it difficult to use stones or mud because of the cold and, therefore, were not undertaking anal-cleansing properly. Also, some people were finding it difficult to excavate mud balls and store them in appropriate places, particularly bearing in mind the coming winter and snow cover in most of the valley.

As a result, some of the community members requested toilet paper, which the implementing agency decided not to provide as, not only did this go against cultural norms, it also provided only a temporary and unsustainable solution. The distribution of sufficient quantities of toilet paper for the whole of the winter to even 1000 families would have been an expensive and complicated matter. Also the problems as articulated by those people requesting toilet paper were not particularly convincing as local people in Panjshir had been managing well enough over countless previous winters. If the problem of storage for mud balls, peculiar to IDPs, was found to be the main issue, then it was agreed that the agency should look into ways of resolving this. Finally, it was decided to distribute plastic sheeting to facilitate outdoor storage.

8.5 Fly reduction

Flies, which tend to breed in areas where human excreta is present, can cause eye infections, particularly among infants and children – and can also be a vector in the transmission of diarrhoeal diseases. They are capable of transmitting dysentery and typhoid, although evidence suggests that they are rarely involved in the transmission of cholera. Flies may also influence whether people are willing to use facilities or not. Between five and ten thousand flies can breed in one kilogram or one litre of organic matter. They usually have a lifespan of one to two months. Fly-control measures include:

- physical screens;
- fly traps;
- lids on latrine squat-holes (except for VIP latrines);
- keeping latrine interiors dark;
- covering faeces with soil, ash or lime;
- regular cleaning of latrines;
- spraying of slab and superstructure with diesel; and
- applying chemical insecticides.

Reducing the number of flies quickly in an emergency can be difficult. Consulting with the affected community on the best method of controlling flies should be a first step in preventative action and, if necessary, educational measures should be promoted where the solutions chosen are unfamiliar. Physical screens or fly traps may be the best immediate measure. Installing vent pipes topped with anti-corrosive screens can reduce flies and smells, and lids should always be provided for squat-holes, except in the case of VIP toilets where a lid should not be used to allow air currents.

Preventative action to eliminate or limit breeding areas and make conditions less favourable to flies is the best long-term solution. Improving personal hygiene along with safe excreta disposal, drainage and garbage disposal will assist in prevention. Cleaning latrines regularly and storing food safely can help prevent the transfer of faecal-oral disease. It may also be relevant to look at the type of latrine model being used – for example, with trench latrines, using excavated soil to cover faeces after each use is recommended.

Chemical insecticides can also be used to kill flies. In general, however, systematic recourse to chemical control should be avoided, as such products are costly and toxic to humans and the environment, and insects can quickly develop resistance to the chemicals used. Insecticides should only be used when absolutely necessary and as a short-term measure. In some cases, small quanties of diesel have been used to spray the superstructure and latrine slab to deter flies. Typically, less than half a decilitre (0.05 litres) per latrine is needed.

Another way to reduce fly populations is to control fly larvae. The following options can be used to prevent fly-larvae growth:

*   using a whitewash of lime and salt on pit walls to prevent the larvae from climbing the walls;

*   regularly adding small amounts of ash, soil or lime to cover faeces;

*   using biological larvicide and other organic products, including pyrethrum flower powder.

8.6 Sludge reduction

Sludge-reducing agents have been developed to speed up the sludge-digestion process. These bioadditives are designed to boost one or more of the three basic ingredients of digestion: nutrients, enzymes and bacteria. If successful, such bioadditives could be added to pit-latrine contents to reduce sludge volumes so that pits can be emptied less frequently.

Several studies testing the effectiveness of various sludge-reduction additives have indicated that some bioadditives are successful in accelerating reductions in sludge volumes and reducing fly infestation. In these trials, however, recorded increases in sludge-reduction rates vary considerably from 5% to 50% – and all studies indicate the need for further testing and research (Redhouse, 2001).

Due to the generally faster rate of sludge accumulation in emergencies, it is not yet known how appropriate such technologies are for emergency excreta disposal programmes. There are also significant constraints to their application, including cost, procurement and, ideally, the need for regular stirring to maximize volume reduction.

Sludge-reduction bioadditives do not increase liquefaction of sludge and, therefore, do not make it any easier to empty latrines by desludging.

8.7 Latrine desludging

Many excreta disposal technology choices involve the construction of a pit or tank which does not rely on infiltration but will need emptying if used in the long-term. Where possible, pits should be appropriately sized or replaced to prevent the need for regular emptying or desludging. This is not always possible, often due to lack of space, and where this is the case facilities for emptying must be in place. Desludging should be considered in situations where:

- land availability is scarce, i.e. it is not possible to dig another pit nearby when one is full;

- ground conditions mean that raised latrines have had to be built: e.g. high water-table, impermeable ground or hard rock areas; or

- latrine pits have been lined, for stability or to prevent groundwater pollution (if the pit is not lined there is a danger of pit collapse when the solids are removed).

If latrines are to be desludged, then either the hole in the squatting-slab needs to be large enough to allow a hose through for pumping; or a removable slab or a removable cover, outside the cubicle, needs to be made to allow a hose or a person to enter. The preferable option is a removable cover so that solids that cannot be pumped out can be dug out and any spillage during desludging does not contaminate the inside of the latrine.

When the contents of the pit or tank are to be pumped out and the sludge is too firm or dry it may be necessary to jet on water and agitate the mixture of sludge and water with the end of the suction hose before pumping begins.

Mechanical emptying

The easiest and most hygienic method for emptying latrines is to use a vacuum tanker (sometimes known as a 'sludge-gulper') which is a truck with a large tank fitted with a mechanical pump. After pumping out the contents of the pit, the tanker can be driven to a safe-disposal site, such as an off-site underground pit or sewage treatment works, where the contents can be emptied. Vacuum tankers are good at removing liquids but poor at removing solid material. Dry pits or pits containing large quantities of solid materials such as stones, sticks, plastic bags, etc. cannot be emptied. Another problem with vacuum tankers is that they are very large and may be difficult to manoeuvre close to latrines.

Where a purpose-built vacuum tanker is unavailable or inappropriate, a collection tank can be mounted on a flat-bed truck, and a portable pump used to pump the waste from the pit to the tank. Such pumps must be carefully selected, particularly where hard anal-cleansing materials are used, and specialist sewage pumps are recommended. Centrifugal desludging pumps are most suitable for wet conditions and, if necessary, a small volume of water can be pumped into the pit first and stirred into the sludge to help liquefy it. Diaphragm desludging pumps which can operate at lower flow rates are also available, and may be more effective in emptying pit latrines than high flow-rate centrifugal pumps.

Electrical submersible sludge pumps can also be used for desludging pit latrines. Such a pump has a metal grill to prevent large bits of rubbish, bottles, bones etc., clogging up and jamming the impeller. If extra pumping head is required these pumps can be put in series. Pumps can be used to pump slurry into ex-water tankers, barrels or metal tanks mounted on flat bed trucks, or tanks for transportation to a disposal area. The aim of this type of desludging is not to remove everything from the latrine – only the slurry component. Removing the top two-thirds of the pit sludge can extend the life of the latrine by a few years before, eventually, the compacted solids will have to be dug out by hand.

Hand-operated latrine-emptying pumps are available in some countries, such as MAPET in Tanzania and Vacutug in Kenya, Bangladesh and Mozambique (for more information see UN-HABITAT, 2006). These are usually mounted on a hand-pushed cart which can be wheeled close to the pit to be emptied. These are much slower than a mechanical pump and some experience is necessary. Such pumps are most appropriate if available and used locally, and where pit contents are wet.

Box 8.2 describes different options used for desludging in Mozambique.

Difficulties encountered in mechanical desludging include:

- difficult vehicular access to latrines;
- dry excreta with little liquid content which cannot be pumped, and lack of available water to dilute pit contents;
- solid anal-cleansing materials which clog up pump or hose;

- difficulty keeping up with demand where there are large numbers of pits that fill rapidly;

- lack of an appropriate site for final disposal of waste; and

- where latrines are inaccessible or poorly maintained, people may choose instead to defecate into plastic bags and throw them into the latrines – this is likely to block up the sludge truck.

In general, it is easier to empty septic-tanks than latrine pits because the septic-tank sludge is much less dense. Consequently, a medium-powered vacuum pump is usually strong enough to lift septic-tank sludge.

Manual emptying

As a last resort, pits can be emptied manually. This generally involves workers climbing into the pit and using shovels and buckets to take the waste out. This can then be placed in a wheelbarrow, or truck, and taken to a safe off-site disposal site. This should only be attempted once a pit has been closed and the contents left to decompose for some time (preferably at least one year and ideally two years). This allows sufficient time for Ascaris (roundworm) eggs, which are the most persistent pathogen, to die off. This period can be shortened by raising the pH (by adding lime or other alkaline material), raising the temperature, or reducing the moisture content.

Although many cultures have a tradition of hand-emptying pits, in densely populated areas this should be avoided if at all possible. It is also important to check with local authorities, as the practice is illegal in some countries.

In Katale Camp, Goma in 1995, latrines were emptied using buckets which were subsequently emptied into 200-litre drums on 3-tonne trucks, which disposed of the material in a dump some 6km away. Approximately 100m^3 sludge for 150,000 people was evacuated every week using this method.

Box 8.2.

Desludging after a flood in Mozambique

In response to the floods in Mozambique in 2000, a large desludging programme was initiated to desludge overflowed septic-tanks during the 2nd phase. This took place in a town with a large IDP population, which had a pre-existing sewerage system servicing houses with septic-tanks. During the floods, the septic-tanks became full with mud and floodwater and had to be emptied quickly.

In this case, there was no desludging truck available, so an electric, submersible sludge pump was ordered. More water was added to the septic-tanks, and a hole was dug away from the tanks, a fair distance from the houses. The team then pumped water from the septic-tank into the hole and afterwards covered it back up with soil, and then dug out the residue at the bottom of the tanks by hand. This option was chosen because access to a truck was unfeasible, and roads were very difficult to access. The pump proved to be particularly useful in this context and didn't jam despite handling large amounts of waste – however this was directly dependent on water being mixed with the waste to increase the liquid content. Previously, the pump had not been tested for desludging.

One of the cheapest methods of desludging is to use a trailer-mounted agricultural muck-spreader which has an in-built vacuum pump, as seen in the photograph (right) in Chokwe, Mozambique.

Box 8.2. continued..

In other programmes in Mozambique the Vacutug (pictured) was used, with the advantage of greater manoeuvrability and easier access to latrines.

Sludge disposal

Sludge that has been left undisturbed for over two years is not a hazard to the environment. It can safely be spread anywhere convenient such as a garden or refuse tip. Its fertilizer value is not good but it will add humus and fibre to the soil which will promote plant growth.

Open disposal of fresh sludge into water or onto land is undesirable – it is an environmental and health hazard. The best solution is to bury sludge in pits where it cannot come into contact with humans or animals, and will not contaminate groundwater sources. Alternatives are to mix it with the influent at a nearby sewage works or compost it with domestic refuse.

Untreated fresh sludge can be used as a fertilizer but great care should be taken to avoid contamination of crops. It is preferable to leave the sludge undisturbed for a long period or to compost it.

For composting, the sludge should be mixed with two or three times its volume of vegetable waste. It is then piled into windrows (long heaps, typically about 2m wide at the top, 2m high, with sides sloping at about 45°) for several weeks. It can then be used as fertilizer.

Sludge can also be disposed of in drying beds. These are usually shallow trenches (about 300mm deep) and should only be used where the groundwater is more than 1.5m below the base of the pit. In permeable conditions this allows the liquids to infiltrate and the sludge can be left to dry so that it can be removed manually. The period it should be left will depend on the temperature, humidity and rainfall, but this should be **at least** two weeks.

8.8 Decommissioning facilities

In some scenarios involving temporary facilities it may be necessary to develop a programme for dismantling and decommissioning excreta disposal facilities. The organization responsible for latrine construction is normally also responsible for decommissioning.

Some key issues to consider in decommisioning are outlined below:

1. Decommissioning should ideally be carried out during the 'dry' season when the pit or tank contents will have had the most opportunity to dry out.

2. Staff should be trained and provided with protective clothing in order to dismantle superstructures, remove latrine slabs and pipes, and backfill pits.

3. Lime or another form of disinfectant should be used to clean latrine slabs or pedestals, and to mitigate against unpleasant odours. It can also be added to latrine contents to aid decomposition, though this is not normally necessary when pits are to be filled and sealed with earth.

4. If the pit contents are wet it may be necessary to dig an overflow trench from the top of the pit or tank to absorb displaced fluids. This should be made large enough to allow a large quantity of material to be placed into the pit or tank. The trench can either be dug around the top of the latrine or out as a single line drain to work as a leach field.

5. Cement debris from the latrine structure or other dismantled facilities can be thrown into the pit along with wood chips, ash or other available organic matter to aid decomposition. As these are added, fluids will overspill into the overflow trench; once the flow stops this can then be backfilled with soil and site rubble.

6. The pit or tank should then be capped with a mound of soil and rubble to allow for further settling of contents.

7. Vegetation can be planted on the latrine site if in line with site rehabilitation. If not, a larger pile of debris should be placed over the filled pit to allow for further subsidence as the contents settle and decompose further. Capping with concrete should be considered if in a populated area where interference is possible.

8. If possible the area should be fenced off to prevent it from being disturbed.

9. Used, prefabricated plastic superstructure units may become a solid waste problem. If these cannot be re-used they should be recycled or disposed of in conjunction with local authorities.

9.

Monitoring

This chapter presents a simple framework for monitoring emergency excreta disposal programmes.

9.1 The need for monitoring

Monitoring is the systematic and continuous process of collecting and using information, throughout the programme cycle, for the purpose of management and decision-making. The process should be started at the beginning of an excreta disposal programme in order to track progress against the objectives – and to make adjustments before it is too late.

Monitoring is often seen as a cumbersome system forced on field staff by managers, donors or headquarters. This is unfortunate, as a good monitoring system can actually help staff to plan their projects. If a good monitoring system is in place, there will be no surprises when an evaluation is carried out.

Other reasons for monitoring could be to:

- look at how objectives are being achieved so that changes can be made – but also to learn from the process (this is useful when planning a new excreta disposal programme);

- look at strengths and weaknesses and to identify spin-offs (unintentional effects) either positive or negative;

- track use of resources – both financial as well as materials;

- make sure the community is involved and that the process is documented;

- make sure that the needs of vulnerable groups such as disabled people are catered for;
- make sure Sphere standards are being maintained (where appropriate); and
- help identify areas for staff training.

9.2   Objectives and indicators

The logical framework is a tool frequently required by donors when funding is being sought. Even if a logframe is not required, it is a good idea to establish objectives, indicators and means of verification right at the beginning of the project. If it is a large project, it is probably a good idea to write up a monitoring strategy with clearly defined roles for who does what, when and how.

Indicators should not just look at activities but also check on outputs (process) and outcomes (impact). This means that it is not enough just to monitor construction but also to look at usage and maintenance as well as user satisfaction. Indicators should be quantitative (numbers) and qualitative (judgement).

Some examples are given below in the logframe in Table 9.1. Process indicators are at output or result level; impacts are at outcome or purpose level as well as at the goal level.

It is worth spending some time on setting indicators that are measurable and realistic: if it is done well at the beginning, useful information can be collected throughout the life of the project.

Baseline indicators may include direct metrics in relation to health and provision of facilities and use, as well as proxy indicators related to well-being, dignity and security.

It is also good practice to divide indicators into 1st phase and 2nd phase indicators as the immediate priorities and outputs are likely to differ to those for the longer term.

Table 9.1. Logframe example

Narrative summary	Measurable indicators	Means of verification	Recorded information
Aim/Goal:			
To contribute to improving the health of the at risk population.	Crude Mortality Rate and morbidity rates from all causes (where possible)	Clinic data Community surveys	*Mortality and morbidity data within accepted limits* *No major outbreaks of communicable diseases in target area* *Perceived reduction in communicable diseases by community members after six months*
Purpose:			
To reduce the incidence of diseases associated with inadequate excreta disposal for population X for Y months.	Mortality and morbidity rates from diarrhoeal diseases (though other external factors may affect morbidity rates) Proxy indicators: • Acceptability of facilities • Use of facilities • Perceived improvements	Clinical data Community surveys Latrine monitoring forms Observation Pocket voting Focus group discussions (FGDs)	*Diarrhoeal mortality and morbidity data within accepted limits* *More than 80% of men, women and children are using and maintaining latrines after 12 months* *The majority (over two-thirds) of women in FGDs express satisfaction[1] with the safety, privacy and accessibility of latrines*

[1] Satisfaction will need to be defined in terms of safety, cleanliness, privacy, dignity, accessibility, suitability, adequacy and other community-defined indicators.

Table 9.1. Logframe example continued...

Narrative summary	Measurable indicators	Means of verification	Important assumptions
Output:			
To ensure adequate excreta disposal in line with Sphere minimum standards within six months. All sections of the community are enabled to practice safer hygiene in a dignified and culturally appropriate manner.	• 1 latrine constructed per 20 people after community consultation OR 1 latrine per household • No faecal matter observed in the target area • Hand washing facilities at all latrines and are maintained • Each household reports the presence of soap on random weekly visits	Latrine-monitoring forms Reports by latrine assistants Observation Weekly, random transect walk Random household visits Handwashing demonstrations with children	*Latrine coverage* *Evidence of faecal matter in the target area* *Number and condition of handwashing facilities* *Proportion of households reporting the presence of soap on random weekly visits*
Activities:			
1. Recruit & train personnel 2. Design & construct latrines 3. Monitor programme activities and indicators...... etc.	Numbers of staff and training completed Etc...	Project records, training evaluation Etc...	*Recruited 1 hygiene promoter per 500 people* *Etc.....*
Inputs:			
	Tools and resources	Logistics and financial records	*50 latrine digging kits distributed etc.....*

When considering Sphere indicators during monitoring it is important to consider their applicability to the specific context under scrutiny. For example, where there is a family latrine programme it is more appropriate to consider the percentage of households with access to improved excreta disposal (rather than the number of people per latrine).

9.3 Monitoring methods

Once the indicators have been set, it is much easier to determine the means of verification: how the information needed will be collected and how often this needs to be done. The system should be put in place as soon as is reasonably possible after the onset of the emergency. It is also good to have some basic baseline data such as people's normal excreta disposal habits, handwashing habits and cultural aspects of excreta disposal. This information is needed in order to provide culturally acceptable facilities.

Some examples of monitoring methods are described below:

- Construction records – a simple form to record the completion of each latrine (household or communal) with a quality-control check. There also needs to be a note made of the community consultation, the number of people consulted and what was the outcome.

- Usage and maintenance records – there are several formats that can be used. Pictorial forms showing such things as presence of flies, smell, proper hole coverage, level of excreta and whether there are any breakages or other damage. These can be used by community volunteers on a weekly basis and can monitor several households or blocks.

- Transect or observation walks are a very simple way of looking at the usage and maintenance of both latrines and handwashing facilities. These walks can be carried out by staff, volunteers or even children. Observations should be recorded and reported on.

- Pocket voting can also be used to monitor latrine use. This process entails holding a community meeting at which attendees (ideally including men, women and children) are asked to indicate whether or not they currently use latrines by placing a bean or tablet in a particular box. This 'voting' should take place in private in order to encourage honesty and obtain an accurate picture of latrine use. This

185

can then be followed up by focus group discussions or informant interviewees to establish **why** latrines are not used.

- Focus groups are a useful tool for finding out such things as community satisfaction and level of involvement. This tool is especially good when talking to vulnerable groups such as the disabled who have very specific needs. But this requires a trained facilitator so that it does not turn into a question and answer session or a large meeting. Data from focus groups should be reported as quotes and never as percentages.

- Activities with children are a good monitoring tool as well as being fun and a learning experience for the children. They can be involved in drawing pictures of defecation habits, they can do small household 'surveys' where they observe family habits over a day or so – or they can do pocket voting. In two projects in Bangladesh and Sierra Leone, children put coloured flags in areas in the community where there was indiscriminate defecation: 'showing and shaming'.

- Community mapping carried out during the assessment (see Chapter 2) can be used later to monitor. A project in post-tsunami India used a map of the facilities to then monitor usage and maintenance using pictures for the illiterate villagers to rate services.

Monitoring should be a joint activity between community members, technicians and the public health promotion team in order to improve the overall effectiveness of the project. Results from monitoring should be shared at regular meetings so that changes can be made or lessons learned.

In the absence of monitoring, latrine 'coverage' figures become largely meaningless. While there may have been a sufficient number of latrines constructed in terms of people per latrine, it is only possible to determine their effectiveness by monitoring latrine condition and usage (see Box 9.1).

Appendix 5 contains examples of latrine-monitoring forms that can be used for monitoring condition and usage.

Box 9.1

Latrine-coverage monitoring in Eastern Chad

Administrative estimates of latrine coverage in Oure Cassoni Camp gave a latrine coverage of 17.5 people per latrine (1600 latrines constructed for a population of 28,000). Although this figure was well within SPHERE excreta disposal guidelines, an increase in diarrhoeal-disease rates and suspected outbreaks of typhoid prompted a comprehensive evaluation of the excreta disposal situation. A GPS-based latrine census-form was used to determine the exact number, location and condition of all latrine infrastructures in the camp. Programme staff visited every public latrine and recorded the following information:

- Latrine type (plastic sheeting or mud block)

- Amount of space left in the latrine pit (verified by shining a torch into the drop-hole)

- Whether plastic sheeting public latrines offered privacy (defined by whether plastic was ripped or not)

- Whether mud-block public latrines offered privacy (defined by whether metal doors were broken or not)

- Cleanliness of the latrine (a dirty latrine was defined as faeces present on slab)

- Whether the drop-hole had a drop-hole cover

- Whether the latrine had a fly-infestation problem (defined as a minimum of two flies entering or exiting the drop-hole in a period of one minute).

A total of 322 three-stance latrine blocks were visited and a major problem was reported with 169 (84%) of the 201 plastic-sheeting latrines requiring urgent repairs to plastic sheeting that had been torn apart by high winds. Revised estimates of latrine coverage – taking into account latrine blocks that had ripped plastic sheeting, were full, or had broken doors – gave a latrine coverage of 41.2 people per latrine.

Monitoring framework

It is good to have a framework or strategy so that everyone knows exactly when and how to monitor. It is not just the technical staff who are responsible for monitoring but everyone involved in the project or programme. See Table 9.2.

Monitoring review

It is useful to have an internal review after a couple of months of implementation. This can be done with the whole team using the SWOT analysis.

SWOT (Strengths, Weaknesses, Opportunities and Threats) analysis is a simple monitoring exercise that can be conducted through brainstorming by all key stakeholders under the following headings:

Strengths: Those things that have worked

Weaknesses: Those things that have not worked so well or could be improved

Opportunities: Conditions which are favourable and can be taken advantage of by the programme

Threats: Threats which reduce the range of opportunities for improvement

The purpose of this exercise is to provide a rapid summary of the key positive and negative aspects of the programme to date. This should help participants to focus on programme successes and how to sustain them, and weaknesses and how to overcome them. The process should also identify spin-offs. The process needs to have a facilitator to lead people otherwise it can be quite subjective and may not look at negative aspects.

Table 9.2. Monitoring framework

Monitoring component	Monitoring data
Staff	Has the target number of staff been recruited and trained?
	Does this include skilled staff from within the affected community?
	How are staff selected and trained? Is training on-going?
	Are staff supervised and appraised?
	Are staff working effectively and efficiently?
	Are there any personnel problems or conflicts?
Resources	Are appropriate resources procured and used as planned?
	Are logistical procedures clear and efficient?
	Is there regular feedback on order status from the logistics department?
	Is there a need for any additional resources?
	Are local materials used where possible?
	Are there any detrimental environmental effects?
Finances	Has the budget been kept to so far, and if not, why not?
	How does expenditure compare with each budget-line forecast?
	Is there regular feedback from the finance department?
	Are there any significant unforeseen costs or savings?
Time	Are activities being implemented according to schedule; if not, why?
	Is time managed efficiently?
	Are there any unforeseen time constraints?
Outputs	Are the targets for facilities and hygiene promotion being met; if not, why not?
	Has the overall health of the population improved?
	Are benefits spread equally among the affected population; is anyone excluded?
	Are the outputs sustainable?
	Are there any relevant needs which have not been addressed?
	Are there any unforeseen effects caused by the programme?

Table 9.2. Monitoring framework continued .....

Monitoring component	Monitoring data
Community	Is the community actively involved in design, construction, O&M?
	Are all facilities being used and if not, why not?
	Are community members satisfied with the facilities provided and what suggestions do they have for improvement?
	Have hygiene practices improved?
	Are there any capacity building activities for the community?
	Are there any conflicts between different stakeholders?
Information	Are regular reports and plans produced and disseminated?
	Is information from reports fed back into the implementation process?
	Are meetings held regularly with key stakeholders?
	Are activities co-ordinated between teams?
	Are activities co-ordinated between implementing agencies?
	Is technical support and information available if required?

9.4 Monitoring reports

All monitoring results should not only be used by staff to improve the programme but they should also be fed into the general programme reporting. The most usual form is the situation report. Table 9.3 shows an example.

Monitoring is an essential tool for ensuring programme quality as well as community satisfaction. Monitoring information will also feed into donor reports, statements to the media, as well as proposals for future funding. It is a way of checking on progress, informing all stakeholders, and of feeding into the evaluation of the programme. If done well and implemented early, it can prove to be an invaluable tool for both managers and technical staff.

Table 9.3. Situation report outline

Location
Agency
Reporting period
Name of reporter(s)
Position of reporter(s)
Overall situation summary (security, population, climate, etc.)
Staff issues (new staff, contracts, salaries, etc.)
Goods received in reporting period
Logistics orders outstanding (order dates)
Expenditure for reporting period
Financial requirements for next reporting period
Time constraints (reasons for delays, etc.)
Activities undertaken during reporting period (report against indicators)
Changes made to existing plans (including reasons)
Beneficiary satisfaction or involvement (qualitative data, e.g. from focus groups)
Tasks outstanding / forthcoming activities
Community issues
Information details (meetings held, data received)
Information requested
Other agencies / stakeholders (news and activities)

Appendix 1.
Measuring Soil Infiltration Rates

The method outlined below (adapted from Davis and Lambert, 2002) gives a general feel for the infiltrative capacity of the soil under test – and provides relevant information for infiltration from soakpits or latrines. Such a test should be undertaken at the same depth as the base of the pit to ensure that the test is not distorted by any variation in material with depth.

Method: Force an open steel cylinder (i.e. without ends) of about 300mm diameter a few centimetres into the soil so that it stands upright. Place an upright ruler or gauge stick marked in millimetres into the cylinder. Fill the cylinder with clean water and measure the fall in water level at convenient intervals (5, 10, 20, 30 minutes) as water infiltrates into the soil.

Interpretation: Determine the infiltration rate during each time period and take the average of the results. This will give a very rough guide to the infiltration rate, which is likely to be all that is required for this application.

The percolation value (or infiltration rate) in mm /day
$$= \frac{\text{drop in level (mm)}}{\text{time (days)}}$$

---

e.g. If the water level drops 12mm in 30 minutes:

Infiltration $=$ 12/30 x 60 x 24 = 576 mm/day
(typical value for sandy loam)

Note: The value in mm/day is always equal to the value in litres/m2/day.

For soakpits or pit latrines to function correctly the infiltration rate for clean water should be at least 120mm/day.

Appendix 2.
WATSAN HIV/AIDS Checklist

Table A2.1. Key questions

Q1. How does the current emergency affect the well-being of people already infected with HIV? *Emergency's effect on people with HIV/AIDS*
Q2. How does HIV/AIDS affect the current emergency and post-emergency rehabilitation? *HIV's effect on emergency*
Q3. What are the implications for humanitarian aid practitioners? *Consequences for policy and practice*

Question 1: How does the emergency affect people with HIV or AIDS?

General escalation of infectious diseases because of poor/no sanitation and increased pathogens in water.

Inability of families affected by HIV to maintain good infection-control standards, to adhere to water-based treatment regimes or to sustain desirable levels of personal hygiene.

Consequently, more rapid health deterioration among children and adults with HIV or AIDS.

Question 2: How do HIV and AIDS affect emergency and rehabilitation responses?

Reduced ability to cope of families affected by HIV because their reserves are already depleted. Thus family and community recovery may take longer.

Sick family members cannot walk long distances to water supply or toilet facilities.

Child-headed households resulting from AIDS.

May not be able to carry larger water rations/operate heavy machinery for pumping water etc.

May not be counted in needs-assessment surveys.

Table A2.1. Key questions continued ...

Question 3: What are the implications for humanitarian aid practitioners?

Ration sizes may vary, e.g. families with sick members might need more water for washing.

Water quality more critical for immune-compromised people.

Location of, and supervision at, water-distribution points, washing facilities and toilets (security from sexual violence e.g. well-lit single-sex toilets located centrally not peripherally – and easy access for sick people).

Programmes administered by women and men.

Families' ability to cope is reduced, e.g. smaller water containers, collective labour, reduced skills.

Priority target groups may be different e.g. may include families with sick members, child-headed households, single women, unaccompanied children.

Increased training/skills and support needs of practitioners because of HIV.

Source: Smith and Dutton, 2004

Appendix 3.
Excreta Disposal Guidelines

These are very brief guidelines developed by the watsan cluster taskforce on what is best practice when constructing latrines for official and spontaneous camps in Pakistan following the 2005 earthquake.

Box A3.1.

Guidelines for best practice

COVERAGE

Sphere indicator: Maximum of 20 people per latrine. (In initial phase aim for 50 p/p/latrine). Separate toilets need to be provided for men and women in the ratio 1:3. Ensure disabled toilets where required for specific users, or occasional facilities in shared blocks, and facilities for children.

POSITION

Toilets should be no more than 50m from dwellings. Pit latrines should be a minimum of 6m from dwellings. Latrines should be at least 30m horizontally from any ground water sources.

Male and female latrine blocks should be placed at a suitable distance from each other as acceptable to the users. Where space does not allow a physical gap between blocks then ensure that the entrances are at the furthest ends from each other.

Dig drainage channel or hump around the latrine to stop surface water entering the pit.

Avoid areas prone to flooding (if no choice build a raised latrine)

If stones/gravels available, cover the soil around latrines (at least entrance area). This helps to keep the surface dry and clean.

Where possible, locate latrine per cluster, block and groups of families. This helps community to take responsibilities and creates opportunities for sustainable care and maintenance.

ACCUMULATION RATES (approx.)

Solids: 0.5 Litres/person/day in emergencies (0.04 - 0.15m^3/person/ year in stable situations)

Liquid: When water is used for anal-cleansing the design figure is 1.3 l/p/d. In the initial phase, before wash areas are constructed, people may wash in latrines in which case the figure could be 8 to 10 l/p/d. Note that in areas with poor seepage this means shallow and highly used latrines, such as those nearest the shelters, may fill up quickly where water is used for anal-cleansing.

OTHER IMPORTANT FACTORS

Ensure water is available for anal-cleansing

Provide handwashing facilities with soap

Special rails, seats, and adequate space in cubicles may be necessary to assist the disabled and elderly.

Ensure doors on latrines are adequate (consultation)

Provide lighting where possible.

Where possible, create sanitation & hygiene enclosure which includes latrines, bathing and, where suitable, special sanitary cloth washing and drying facilities for women.

OPERATION AND MAINTENANCE

If the users are not consulted about the siting and design of the latrines they are less likely to use them. Always consult.

Communal latrines: Ensure somebody is responsible for maintaining and regularly cleaning latrines; without a designated person(s), provided with cleaning equipment and regular follow-up and supervision, the latrine programme will fail.

Family latrines: After the initial emergency phase, assign groups of families (4 or 5) to designated latrines. This will be more difficult to implement for large blocks of latrines. Make them responsible for keeping it clean. Allocated families may want to use padlock and key. A cemented plinth and extended floor makes it easier to keep the latrine slabs and bathing floor clean.

MONITORING

Always monitor that the latrines are being used; if not, find out why and address the issue. Monitor cleanliness of latrines and enclosed environment, presence of flies, level of smells, condition of pits and functions of drainage and soakaway facilities. A simple check-sheet can be used for regular sanitary inspection. In this case, latrine and bathing blocks need to be numbered/named.

Appendix 4.
Bills of Quantities

A4.1 Deep trench latrines

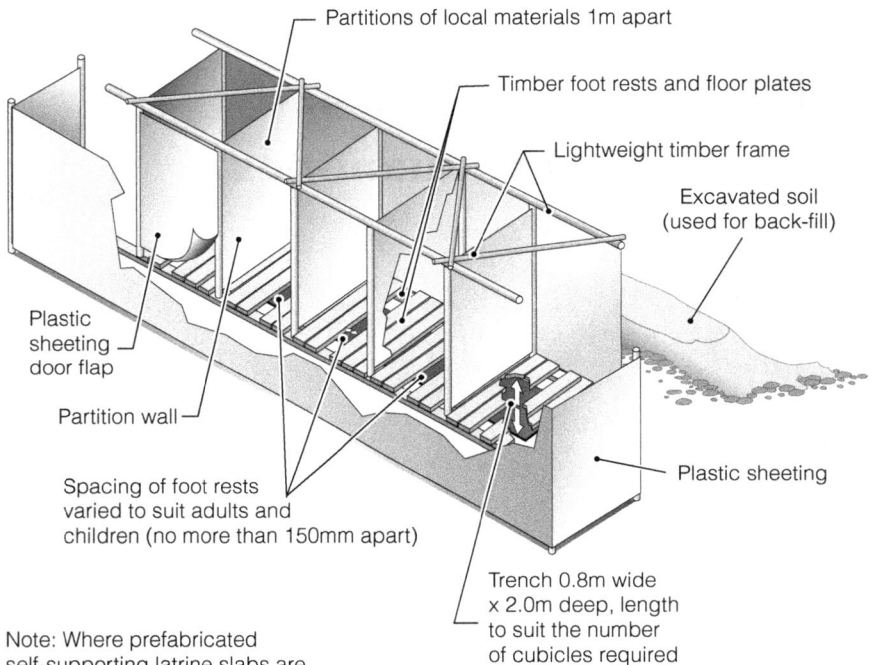

Partitions of local materials 1m apart

Timber foot rests and floor plates

Lightweight timber frame

Excavated soil
(used for back-fill)

Plastic
sheeting
door flap

Partition wall

Spacing of foot rests
varied to suit adults and
children (no more than 150mm apart)

Plastic sheeting

Trench 0.8m wide
x 2.0m deep, length
to suit the number
of cubicles required

Note: Where prefabricated
self-supporting latrine slabs are
to be used in place of timber
cubicle sizes may need to be
adjusted to fit slab width
(e.g. 0.8m)

Superstructure

Table A4.1. BoQ: Deep trench latrine (4-unit block)

Dimensions	Length (m)	Width (m)	Depth (m)
Excavation of trench	4.00	0.80	2.00
Superstructure	**Unit**	**Quantity**	**Linear metric length (m)**
Timber 50 x 50 x 2300mm RT	front post	5	11.50
Timber 50 x 50 x 2100mm RT	back post	5	10.50

Dimensions	Length (m)	Width (m)	Depth (m)
Timber: 50 x 25 x 1200mm RT	cross tie	5	6.00
Timber: 50 x 25 x 1800mm RT	diagonal tie	5	9.00
Timber: 75 x 25 x 4000mm RT	long tie (bottom)	2	8.00
Timber: 75 x 25 x 4000mm RT	long tie (top)	2	8.00
Galvanized-wood nails 2"	No.	40	
Galvanized-wood nails 1"	No.	186	
Bottle tops or folded plastic pads	No.	226	
Plastic sheeting (2m wide x 1m long)	walls	10	10.00
Plastic sheeting (2m wide x 1m long)	door	4	4.00
Slab and supports			
Timber: 15 x 100 x 4000mm RT	support planks	2	8.00
Wooden Slab: 1m x 1.2m	slab	4	
Roof			
Timber: 38 x 50 x 1800mm RT	rafter	5	9.00
Timber: 25 x 25 x (4000+400) mm RT	purlin	3	13.20
Plastic sheeting (2m wide x 1m long)	roof	4.8	4.80
Bottle tops or folded plastic pads	No.	86	
Galvanized-wood nails 1"	No.	86	
Privacy screen (optional)			
Timber 50 x 50 x 2300mm RT	posts	5	11.50
Plastic sheeting (2m wide x 1m long)	screen	8	8.00
Bottle tops or folded plastic pads	No.	52	
Galvanized-wood nails 1"	No.	52	

A4.2 Simple pit latrine (with different superstructure options)

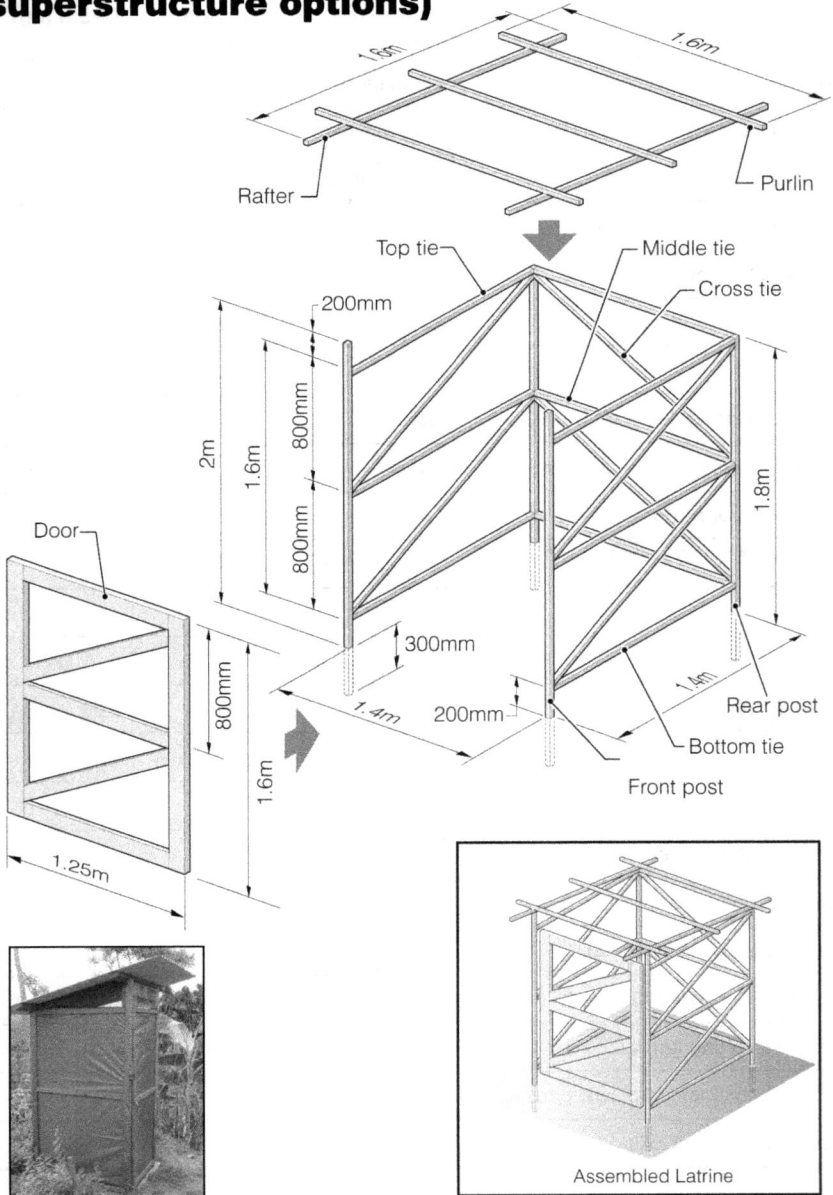

Rafter

Purlin

1.6m

1.6m

Top tie

Middle tie

Cross tie

200mm

2m

1.6m

800mm

800mm

800mm

1.8m

Door

800mm

1.6m

1.25m

300mm

1.4m

200mm

1.4m

Rear post

Bottom tie

Front post

Assembled Latrine

Table A4.2. BoQ: Simple pit latrine
(with different superstructure options)

Dimensions	Depth (m)	Diameter (m)	
Excavation of pit	3.00	0.80	
Superstructure frame	**Unit**	**Quantity**	**Linear metric length (m)**
Timber: 50 x 50 x 2300mm RT	front post	2	4.60
Timber: 50 x 50 x 2100mm RT	back post	2	4.20
Timber: 38 x 25 x 1750mm RT	cross tie	6	10.50
Timber: 50 x 50 x 1300mm RT	bottom tie	3	3.90
Timber: 38 x 50 x 1300mm RT	middle tie	3	3.90
Timber: 50 x 50 x 1300mm RT	top tie	3	3.90
Galvanized-wood nails 2"	No.	30	
Door frame			
Timber: 38 x 50 x 1600mm RT	uprights	2	3.20
Timber: 38 x 50 x 1400mm RT	cross tie	2	2.80
Timber: 38 x 50 x 1150mm RT	horizontal ties	3	3.45
Hinges	No.	3	
Wood screws (1.5")	No.	18	
Galvanized-wood nails 2"	No.	10	
Roof			
Timber: 38 x 50 x 2000mm RT	rafter	2	4.00
Timber: 25 x 25 x 1800mm RT	purlin	3	5.40
Corrugated-iron sheeting (2m x 1.8m wide)	roof	1	
Galvanized-roofing nails	No.	8	

**Table A4.2. BoQ: Simple pit latrine
(with different superstructure options)** continued .....

Slab			
Domed-concrete slab (1.2m diameter) OR Reinforced-concrete slab: 1m x 1.2m OR Self-supporting plastic (Oxfam) slab: 0.8m x 1.2m	slab	1	
Superstructure: CORRUGATED IRON			
Corrugated-iron sheeting (1.6m x 1.4m wide)	walls	3	
Corrugated-iron sheeting (1.6m x 1.2m wide)	door	1	
Galvanized-roofing nails	No.	36	
Superstructure: WOODEN SLATS			
Timber: 75 x 15 x 1400 mm RT	walls	66	92.40
Timber: 75 x 15 x 1250 mm RT	door	22	27.50
Galvanised wood nails 1.5"	No.	176	
Superstructure: PLASTIC SHEETING			
Plastic sheeting (2m wide x 1m long)	walls	4.2	4.20
Plastic sheeting (2m wide x 1m long)	door	1.3	1.30
Bottle tops or folded plastic pads	No.	88	
Galvanized-wood nails 1"	No.	88	

A4.3 Concrete-block-lined single pit (for use with simple pit or VIP latrine)

Table A4.3. BoQ: Concrete-block-lined single pit

Designation	Depth (m)	Diameter (m)
Excavation of pit	3.00	0.8
Concrete blocks (pit internal diameter 0.8m)	**Unit**	**Quantity**
Blocks: 400 x 200 x 100mm	*blocks per row*	*6.28 (7)*
Blocks: 400 x 200 x 100mm	*no. rows*	*15*
Blocks: 400 x 200 x 100mm	No.	105
Cement	25kg bag	1
Building sand	m³	0.25
Latrine slab (SanPlat 1.0m diameter)		
Cement	25kg bag	1
Building sand	m³	0.25
Gravel	m³	0.50

A4.4　Blair VIP latrine

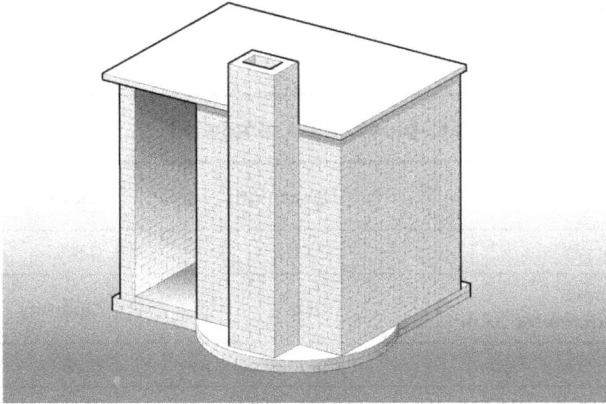

Isometric view of slab and structure

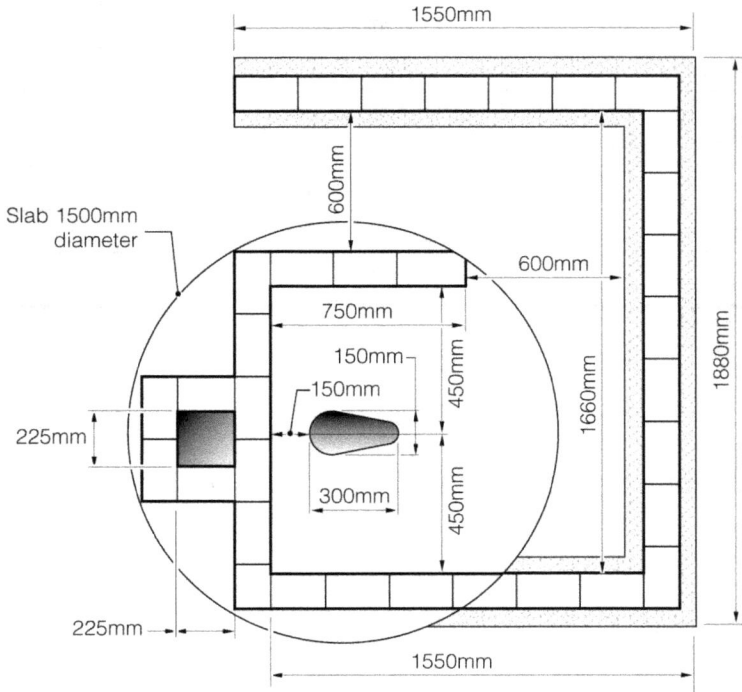

1550mm

600mm

Slab 1500mm
diameter

600mm

750mm

150mm
150mm

450mm

1660mm

1880mm

225mm

300mm

450mm

225mm

1550mm

Plan view of slab and structure

Table A4.4. BoQ: VIP latrine*

Dimensions	Depth (m)	Diameter (m)
Excavation of pit	4.00	1.0
Superstructure and pit-lining	**Unit**	**Quantity**
Cement	25kg bag	4
Building bricks	No.	~1000
River sand	m³	0.5
Pit sand	m³	1.5
Gravel	m³	0.125
Roof		
Cement	25kg bag	1
Chicken wire (1.7m x 2.0m)	m²	3.4
Latrine slab		
Cement	25kg bag	1
Domed-concrete slab (1.2m diameter) *including 150mm-diameter hole for vent pipe*	No.	1
OR Reinforcement wire (3mm) *for reinforced, flat circular slab*	metre	25
Vent Pipe		
PVC pipe (150mm diameter) *or use building bricks*	metre	2.5
Stainless steel or aluminium fly screen: 180mm diameter	screen	1

* Adapted from Morgan (1990)

A4.5 Pour-flush latrine, septic-tank and soakaway

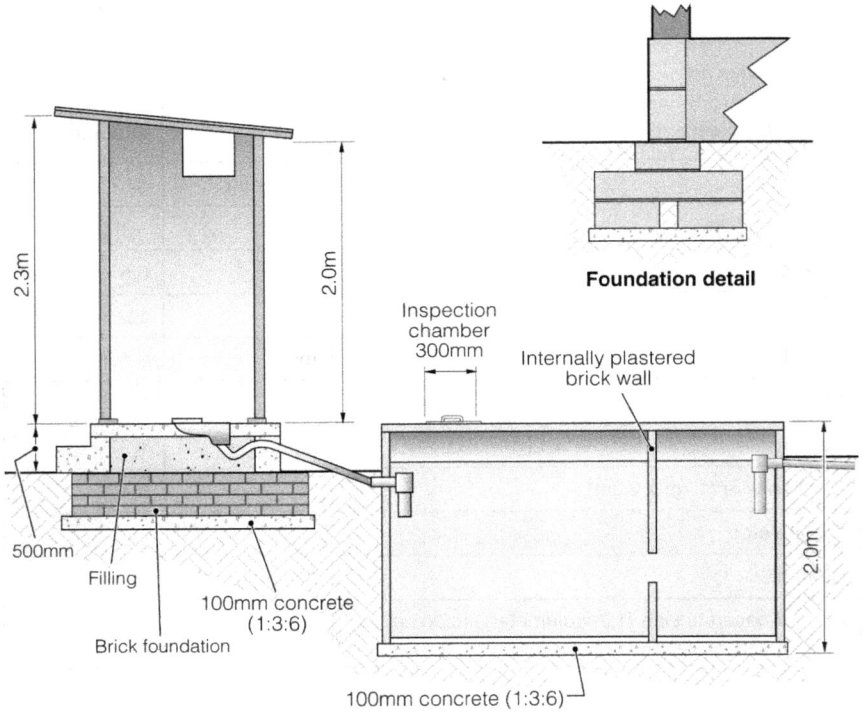

Foundation detail

Side elevation labels: 2.3m, 2.0m, 500mm, Filling, 100mm concrete (1:3:6), Brick foundation, Inspection chamber 300mm, Internally plastered brick wall, 2.0m, 100mm concrete (1:3:6)

Side elevation

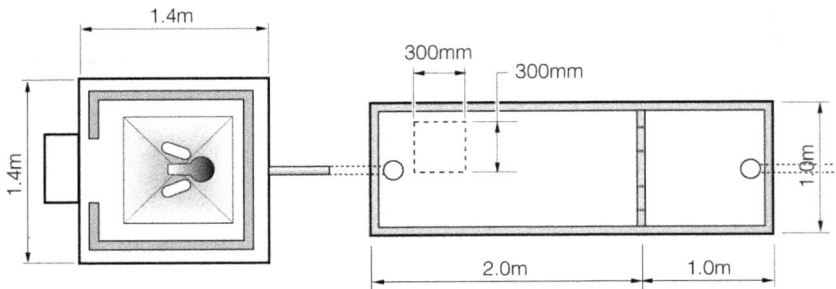

Plan view labels: 1.4m, 1.4m, 300mm, 300mm, 1.0m, 2.0m, 1.0m

Plan view

Table A4.5. BoQ: Pour-flush latrine and septic-tank

Foundation and superstructure	Unit	Quantity
100 x 200 x 400mm cement block	No.	170
20mm (3/4") aggregate	No.	0.15
Silicon gun	tube	0.2
River sand	m³	0.6
Cement	25kg bag	5
Squatting pan with foot-rest	No.	1
Roof		
1.8m corrugated-tin sheet 18 gauge	No.	3
50 x 75mm timber	metre	7
Wire nail	kg	0.3
Cap nail	kg	0.3
Door		
1.8m corrugated-tin sheet 18 gauge	No.	1
150mm (6") tail hinge	No.	2
100mm (4") towel bolt	No.	1
Screw nail 20mm (3/4")	No.	16
Wire nail	kg	0.2
Cap nail	kg	0.3
50 x 75mm timber	metre	6
50 x 50mm timber	metre	7
Septic-tank and soakage pit		
Building bricks	No.	1500
River sand	m³	0.5
Cement	25kg bag	6
20mm (3/4") aggregate	m³	0.3
110mm PVC T	No.	1
110mm PVC pipe	metre	4.5
Rebar (10mm)	metre	32.0

A4.6 Double-vault, urine-diverting latrine

150mm Ø
100mm Ø
580mm
200mm
350mm
350mm
350mm
R1
0.15m
500m

View on arrow 'A'

2.0m
300mm
300mm
1.4m
2.0m
2.8m

A

Urinal and washing
water outlet

0.8m
G.L.
0.5m
1.8m

Table A4.6. BoQ: Double-vault, urine-diverting latrine

Dimensions	Depth (m)	Length (m)	Width (m)
Excavation of foundations	0.50	2.5	2.5
Superstructure, Chamber & Roof (Complete)	**Unit**	**Quantity**	
Cement	25kg bag	8.8	
Red-cement powder	kg	0.5	
Sand	m³	53	
Rubble (approx. 150mm x 300mm)	m³	42	
Aggregate 20mm (3/4")	m³	12	
Blocks (400mm x 200mm x 100mm)	No.	314	
Rebar 10mm diameter	metre	36	
Binding wire	kg	0.3	
Door			
Door – complete with frame	unit	1	
Hinges	No.	3	
Bolt (internal)	No.	1	
Padlock + padlock hinge	No.	1	
Wood screws (1.5 inch)	No.	24	
Squat-plate	unit	2	
Urine Separation Plumbing			
PVC pipe 50 mm (2") diameter	metre	3	
PVC "T" socket 50 mm (2")	No.	1	
PVC 50 mm (2") x 90° bend	No.	1	
PVC pipe 110 mm (4") diameter	metre	4	
PVC "T" socket	No.	1	
PVC 110 mm (4") x 90° bend	No.	2	

A4.7 Double-unit pit latrine

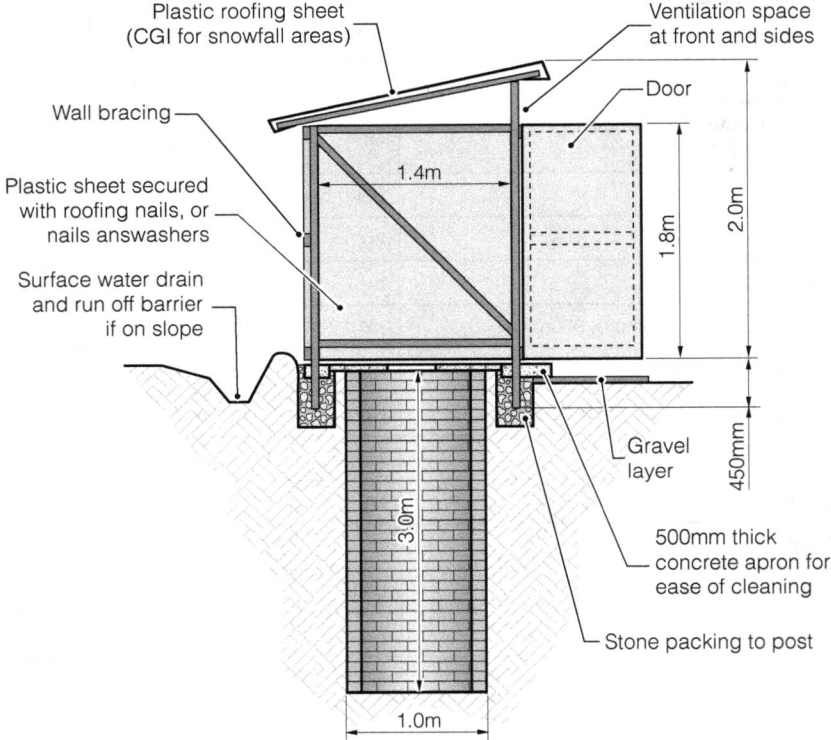

Plastic roofing sheet
(CGI for snowfall areas)

Ventilation space
at front and sides

Door

Wall bracing

Plastic sheet secured
with roofing nails, or
nails answashers

Surface water drain
and run off barrier
if on slope

1.4m

1.8m

2.0m

450mm

3.0m

1.0m

Gravel
layer

500mm thick
concrete apron for
ease of cleaning

Stone packing to post

Side view

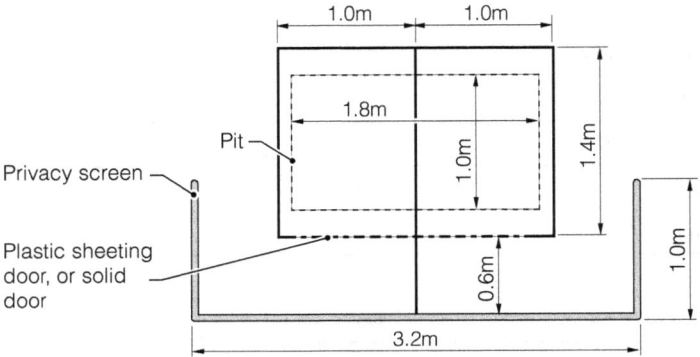

1.0m   1.0m

1.8m

1.0m

1.4m

Pit

Privacy screen

Plastic sheeting
door, or solid
door

0.6m

1.0m

3.2m

Plan view

214

Table A4.7. BoQ: Double-unit pit latrine

Dimensions	Depth (m)	*Length (m)*
Excavation of Pit	3.00	2.00
Detail of Items	**Unit**	**Quantity**
Wooden posts 50 x 50 x 2400mm	piece	6
Wooden posts 50 x 50 x 2100mm	piece	2
Wooden plank 75 x 15 x 2400mm	piece	3
Plastic latrine slab: 0.8 x 1.2m	No.	2
CGI sheet	No.	2
Steel twisting (10mm diameter)	metre	6
Plastic sheeting (2.0m width)	metre	8
Wooden posts 50 x 75 x 2800mm	No.	6
Nails 1", 3" and 4" (200gm each)	kg	0.6

A4.8 Women's hygiene unit

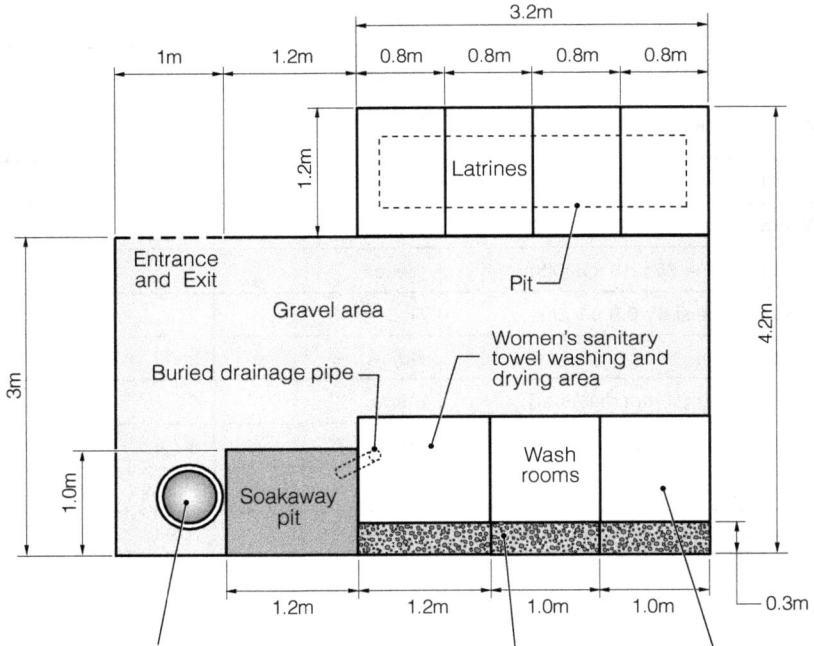

Hand-washing barrel with tap and soap (broken into pieces to try and prevent it being stolen, and hung in a sock or small sack tied to the hand washing barrel).

The barrel should ideally be standing on the soak-pit and near to the exit door of the screened areas (as a reminder for people to wash their hands).

Stone filled drainage channel which should be within the wash room units and under the covered roof area.

Sloping concrete or marble slabs placed on a bed of sand, with smooth finish for easy cleaning.

Table A4.8. BoQ: Women's hygiene unit

Detail	Unit	Quantity
Wooden posts 50 x 50 x 2400mm	No.	14
Wooden posts 50 x 50 x 2100mm	No.	9
Wood 50 x 25 x 2400mm – used for cross bars and bracings for latrines, bath units and screens	No.	36
Wood 150 x 50 x 1600mm – wooden frame for supporting the latrine slabs at the top of the pit	No.	9
Small gravel chippings – no fines – for the ground surface, the stone drain for bath units and the top of the soakpits	m³	0.6
Large stones / rocks for filling soakpit	m³	1.2
Tarpaulin / plastic sheeting (thick, ideally coloured / not white, with fabric weave where possible)	m²	100
'Washels' (washers to use with standard 2" nails – could be replaced with roofing nails, or rubber washers)	kg	3
Nails 3"	kg	1
Nails 2"	kg	5
Nails 1"	kg	1
Binding wire – for door locks and additional bracing for screen if required	kg	2
Sand – for bedding to form the slope for the marble bathing slabs and for constructing the edging for the hygiene unit	m³	0.5
0.8m x 1.2m Oxfam slabs (produced in India)	No.	4
1.0m x 1.2m x 20mm (¾") marble sheets – with rough surface – for bath units and base of hygiene unit	No.	3
Cement – for plastering brick edges to hygiene unit and forming connection to uPVC pipe outlet	25kg bag	0.5
Burnt bricks – for constructing edging for the hygiene unit to direct water into the pipe	No.	30
90mm (3") UPVC pipe	metre	0.5

A4.9 Septic-tank

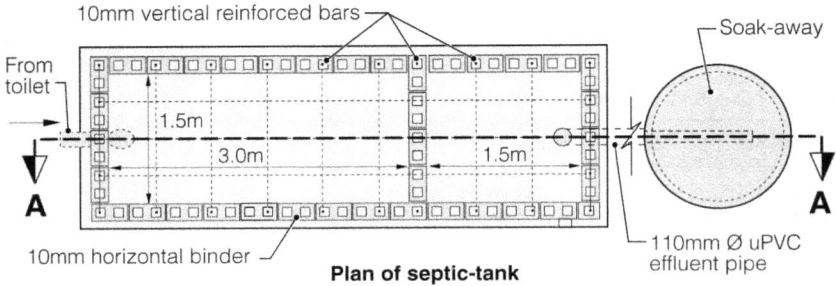

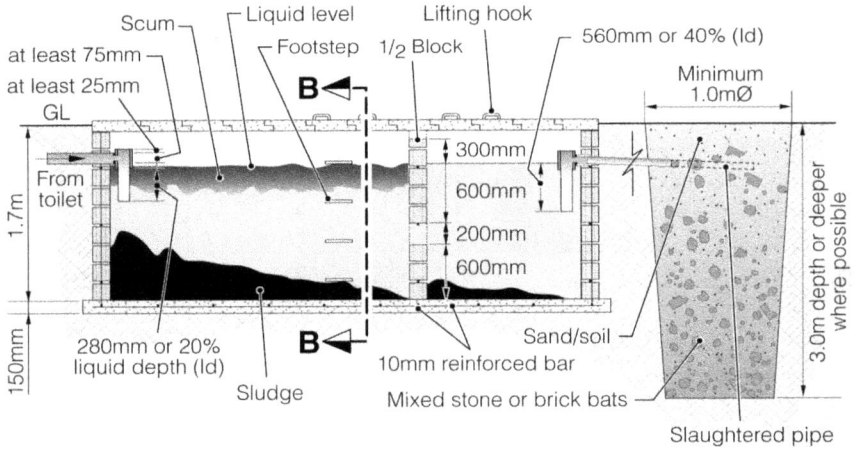

10mm vertical reinforced bars

From toilet

1.5m

3.0m

1.5m

Soak-away

A

A

10mm horizontal binder

110mm Ø uPVC effluent pipe

Plan of septic-tank

Scum

Liquid level

Lifting hook

1/2 Block

560mm or 40% (ld)

Footstep

at least 75mm

at least 25mm

GL

B

Minimum 1.0mØ

300mm

600mm

From toilet

200mm

1.7m

600mm

3.0m depth or deeper where possible

150mm

280mm or 20% liquid depth (ld)

B

Sand/soil

10mm reinforced bar

Mixed stone or brick bats

Sludge

Slaughtered pipe

Section on A-A reinforced in unstable soil

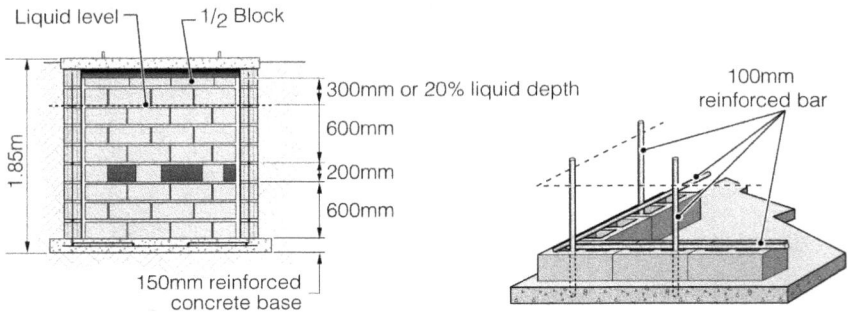

Liquid level

1/2 Block

300mm or 20% liquid depth

600mm

100mm reinforced bar

1.85m

200mm

600mm

150mm reinforced concrete base

Section on B-B

Reinforcement details

218

Table A4.9. BoQ: Reinforced-concrete septic-tank

Tank structure	Unit	Quantity
Cement (casting and plastering)	25kg bag	12
Sand	m³	0.5
Gravel (20mm)	m³	0.3
10mm reinforcing steel bar	metre	100
400 x 200 x 100mm concrete blocks	No.	350
Lifting hooks	No.	4
Pipe and fittings		
100mm-diameter PVC pipe	m	24
100mm PVC flexible coupling	No.	6
100mm PVC screw-end caps	No.	2
100mm PVC tee	No.	4
100mm PVC puddle flanges	No.	7
Vent valves	No.	2
PVC glue	tube	6

A4.10 Sewerage network and infiltration system for five houses

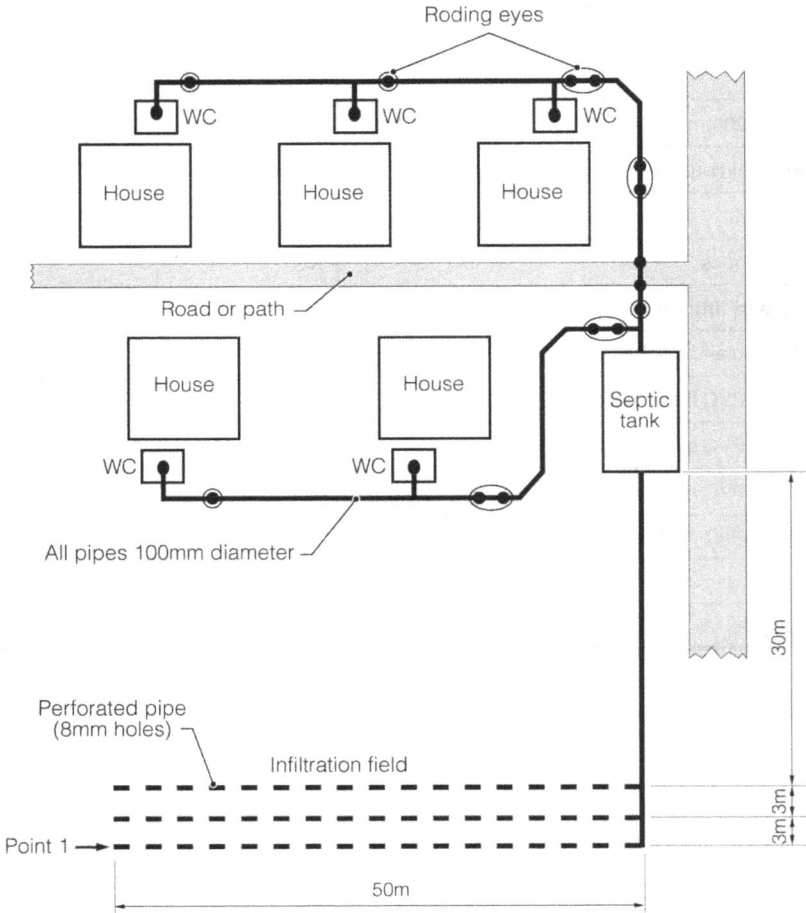

Roding eyes

WC

House

WC

House

WC

House

Road or path

House

House

WC

WC

Septic tank

All pipes 100mm diameter

Perforated pipe
(8mm holes)

Infiltration field

Point 1

50m

30m

3m 3m

| | Single roding eyes |
| | Double roding eyes |

Table A4.10. BoQ: Sewerage network and infiltration system for five houses

Sewerage-pipe network	Unit	Quantity
100mm-diameter PVC pipe	m	120
100mm PVC 90° elbow	No.	5
100mm PVC 45° elbow	No.	25
Flow junction (67°)	No.	13
100mm PVC screw-end caps	No.	12
100mm PVC Tee	No.	1
Cement	25kg bag	6
Sand	m³	0.35
Gravel	m³	0.7
Plywood (9mm x 1.3m x 2.4m)	No.	1
Timber (75mm x 50mm x 2.0m)	piece	5
6m lengths of twisted, 12mm reinforcing-steel bar	No.	3
16 gauge tie wire	kg	0.5
3" nails	kg	0.5
1" nails	kg	0.25
Infiltration system		
100mm PVC screw-end caps	No.	9
100mm diameter PVC pipe *150m of pipe will be perforated with 8mm holes*	m	186
100mm PVC 90° elbow	No.	1
100mm PVC Tee	No.	2
Round gravel (30mm diameter)	m³	90
Sand	m³	8
Palm fibre (for dividing layer between topsoil and infiltration gravel)	kg	200

Appendix 5.

Latrine-monitoring Forms

1) Institution/settlement: _____

2) Location/address: _____

3) Name of interviewee(s): _____

4) Number of facilities?

Latrines	
Urinals	
Handwashing	

5) Number of latrines/urinals observed being used (based on visual inspections)?

Male	Female	Mixed
LATRINES		

Male	Female	Mixed
URINALS		

Where there is more than one latrine the number of positive or negative responses can be written in the respective boxes for Yes (Y) or No (N).

6) Were doors locked on arrival?   Y ☐   N ☐

7) If yes, why? _____

8) Does the latrine show evidence of use?   Y ☐   N ☐

9) If yes, is the pit/chamber observed to be (inspect with torch)

Hardly Used	¼ Full	½ Full	¾ Full	Nearly Full

10)   Are the vault contents wet?   Y [ ]   N [ ]

11)   Have latrines been emptied yet?   Y [ ]   N [ ]

If yes, have chambers been resealed?   Y [ ]   N [ ]

12)   Was it difficult to empty the latrines?   Y [ ]   N [ ]

If so, why_____

13)   How much did it cost to empty the latrines? _____

14)   What is the observed condition of the latrines?

	No	Small Amount	Large Amount
Are faeces visible?			
Are flies present?			
Do latrines smell?			

15) Has the toilet slab/pedestal been fouled
(based on visual inspection)?   Y ☐   N ☐

16) Is the slab/pedestal considered hygienic
to use?   Y ☐   N ☐

If no, observations?_____

17) Is the area around the latrine
(in front and behind) clean?   Y ☐   N ☐

If no, observations?_____

18) Is the water source operational?   Y ☐   N ☐

If no, explain? _____

19) Distance to main water source from latrine? _____ metres

20) Is there water at the hand- washing point ?   Y ☐   N ☐

If no, explain?   _____

21) Is there soap at handwashing point?   Y ☐   N ☐

22) Condition of other elements? (photograph defects)

	Good	Broken
Roof		
Vent pipe		
Door		
Door hinges		
Walls		
Chamber		
Steps		

24) Other information / summary of observations

Date: _____ Interviewer:_____

Latrine-monitoring matrix (for communal pit latrines)

No.	Zone/ Area	Type of latrine	Space left in pit (metres)	Latrine dirty? (Y/N)	Presence of flies? (Y/N)	Drop-hole covered? (Y/N)	Superstructure condition (walls, doors etc.)

References and Bibliography

Adams, John (Ed.) (1995) *Sanitation in Emergency Situations: Proceedings of an international workshop.* Oxfam: Oxford.

Adams, John (1999) *Managing Water Supply and Sanitation in Emergencies.* Oxfam: Oxford.

Almedom, Astier M., Blumenthal, Ursula and Manderson, Lenore (1997) *Hygiene Evaluation Procedures: Approaches and methods for assessing water and sanitation-related practices.* London School of Hygiene and Tropical Medicine (LSHTM) and International Nutrition Foundation for Developing Countries (INFDC): London.

ARGOSS (2001) *Guidelines for assessing the risk to groundwater from on-site sanitation.* British Geological Survey Commissioned Report CR/01/142. 97pp.

Assar, M. (1971) *Guide to Sanitation in Natural Disasters.* WHO: Geneva.

Boot, Marieke T. and Cairncross, Sandy (1993) *Actions Speak: The study of hygiene behaviour in water and sanitation projects.* IRC: Hague, The Netherlands.

Brandberg, Bjorn (1997) *Latrine Building: A handbook for implementation of the SanPlat system.* Intermediate Technology Publications: London.

Chalinder, Andrew (1994) *Good practice review 1: Water and sanitation in Emergencies.* Overseas Development Institute: London.

Curtis, V. and Cairncross, S. (2003) 'Effect of washing hands with soap on diarrhoea risk in the community: A systematic review' in *The Lancet Infectious Diseases*, Vol 3, May 2003, pp 275-281.

Curtis, Valerie (1999) *Hygiene Promotion.* WELL Technical Brief. http://www.lboro.ac.uk/well/services/tecbriefs/hygiene.htm

Davis, Jan and Lambert, Robert (2002) *Engineering in Emergencies: A practical guide for relief workers.* RedR/ IT Publications: London.

Deverill, P.A. and Still, D.A. (1998) *Building School VIPs: Guidelines for the design and construction of ventilated improved pit toilets and associated facilities for schools.* Partners in Development: Pietermaritzburg, South Africa.

Esrey, S. A. (1996) 'Water, waste and well-being: a multicountry study'. *American Journal of Epidemiology,* 143, pp 608-623.

Fewtrell, L., Kaufmann, R.B., Kay, D., Enanoria, W., Haller, L. and Colford Jr., J.M. (2005) Water, sanitation, and hygiene interventions to reduce diarrhoea in less-developed countries: a systematic review and meta-analysis. *The Lancet Infectious Diseases,* Vol 5, pp 42-52.

Feacham, Richard G. et al. (1983) *Sanitation and Disease: Health aspects of excreta and wastewater management.* World Bank: Bath, UK.

Ferron, Suzanne; Morgan, Joy and O'Reilly, Marion (2006*) Hygiene Promotion: From relief to development.* Intermediate Technology Development Group Publishing: UK.

Franceys, R., Pickford, J. and Reed, R. (1992) *A Guide to the Development of On-site Sanitation.* WHO: Geneva.

Gosling, Louisa and Edwards, Mike (1995) *Toolkits: A practical guide to assessment, monitoring, review and evaluation.* Save the Children: London.

Harries, S.D. (2004) *Getting a Handle on Handwashing: Implementation in Emergency Situations.* Unpublished MSc Dissertation, WEDC, Loughborough University: UK.

Harvey, P.A., Baghri, S. and Reed, R.A. (2002) *Emergency Sanitation: Assessment and programme design.* WEDC, Loughborough University: UK. (http://www.wedc.ac.uk)

IASC (2003) *Guidelines for HIV/AIDS Interventions in Emergency Settings (DRAFT)* Inter-Agency Standing Committee.

Jacelon, C.S., Connelly, T.W., Brown, R., Proulx, K. and Vo, T. (2004) 'A concept analysis of dignity for older adults'. *Journal of Advanced Nursing* Vol 48, No 1, pp 76-83.

Jones, H.E. and Reed, R.A. (2005) *Water Supply and Sanitation for Disabled People and other Vulnerable Groups: Designing services to improve accessibility.* WEDC, Loughborough University: UK.

Jones, H.E., Parker, K.J. and Reed, R.A. (2002) *Water supply and sanitation access and use by physically disabled people: A literature review.* WEDC, Loughborough University: UK.

Kalbermatten, John M. and Gunnerson, Charles G. (1985) *Appropriate Technology for Water Supply and Sanitation: A sanitation field manual.* World Bank.

Médecins Sans Frontières (1994) *Public Health Engineering in Emergency Situations.* Médecins Sans Frontières: Paris.

Médecins Sans Frontières (1997) *Refugee Health: An approach to emergency situations.* Médecins Sans Frontières, Macmillan Education Ltd: London and Basingstoke.

Morgan, P. (1990) *Rural Water Supplies and Sanitation.* Macmillan, London, UK.

Oxfam (2001) *Guidelines for Public Health Promotion in Emergencies.* Oxfam Humanitarian Department, Oxfam GB: Oxford.

Oxfam (2000) *Guidelines for excreta disposal in Emergencies.* Oxfam Humanitarian Department, Oxfam GB: Oxford.

Pacey, A. (ed.) (1978) *Sanitation in Developing Countries.* John Wiley & Sons, Chichester, UK.

Peterson, E.A., Roberts, L., Toole, M.J. and Peterson, D.E. (1998) 'The effect of soap distribution on diarrhoea: Nyamithuthu Refugee Camp'. *International Journal of Epidemiology* Vol 27, No 3, pp 520-524.

Redhouse, David (2001) *Less Lump per Dump: Prolonging the life of pit latrines.* Unpublished MSc Dissertation, Cranfield University: Silsoe, UK.

Rottier, E. and Ince, M.E. (2003) *Controlling and Preventing Disease: The role of water and environmental sanitation interventions.* WEDC, Loughborough University: UK.

Smith, Ann and Dutton, Al (2004) *Water Supply and Sanitation and HIV/AIDS*. Presentation to Interagency Environmental Health Forum, CAFOD. (http://www.lshtm.ac.uk/dcvbu/ehg/ann_smith.htm)

Sphere Project (2004) *Humanitarian Charter and Minimum Standards in Disaster Response*. Standing Committee for Humanitarian Response (SCHR): Geneva (http://www.sphereproject.org)

Sugden, S. (2006) *Assessing the Health Risks of Ecological Sanitation*. WELL Report, London School of Hygiene and Tropical Medicine: London, UK.

Toole, M.J. and Waldman, R.J. (1997) *The Public Health Aspects of Complex Emergencies and Refugee Situations*. Annual Review of Public Health Vol 18, USA.

UNCHS (1986) *Community Participation in Low-cost Sanitation*. United Nations Centre for Human Settlements (Habitat): Nairobi.

UN-HABITAT (2006) *The UN-HABITAT Vacutug Project*. UN-HABITAT: Nairobi. (http://hq.unhabitat.org/programmes/vacutug/Overview.asp)

UNHCR (2000) *Handbook for Emergencies*. UNHCR: Geneva.

UNICEF (1998) *Happy, Healthy and Hygienic: How to set up a hygiene promotion programme*. United Nations Children's Fund: New York.

Veer, T. de (1998) *Beyond Sphere: Integral Quality System for Operation of Water and Sanitation Programs in Camps*. Unpublished draft report, De Veer Consultancy: Leiden, The Netherlands.

Walton-Knight, M. (2002) *Emergency Sanitation – A Universal Discharge Consent Standard for Deployable Sewage Treatment Equipment*. Unpublished thesis for MSc in Water Management, Cranfield University: Silsoe, UK.

WHO (1998) *PHAST Step-by-step Guide: A participatory approach for the control of diarrhoeal disease*. WHO: Geneva.

WHO (2006) *The World Health Report 2006 – Working together for health*. WHO: Geneva.

Wisner, B. and Adams, J. (2002) Environmental Health in Emergencies and Disasters: A practical guide. WHO: Geneva.